This book truly has something for everyone, especially if they want to be happy!

Larry Brooks realized that he was a very contented person. So, when he retired, he found the precious time to write his memoirs describing his legacy of love and happiness.

This fascinating and absorbing book follows Larry's life, told in stories. It is also a great piece of social history, describing everyday life and famous events from the baby-booming latter half of the twentieth century through to the present day. It is written with insight, depth, humour and love.

The book is full of true tales, without exaggeration or embellishments, and the learning experiences that have brought Larry much happiness. He wants to share this journey with you.

If this story increases your own happiness, then his mission is complete.

Happy As Larry

My Life and Legacy

Larry Brooks

authorHOUSE®

AuthorHouse™ UK Ltd.
500 Avebury Boulevard
Central Milton Keynes, MK9 2BE
www.authorhouse.co.uk
Phone: 08001974150

First published by AuthorHouse 4/12/2010

ISBN: 978-1-4490-9114-9 (sc)
ISBN: 978-1-4490-9113-2 (hc)

This book is printed on acid-free paper.

This book celebrates
the memory of Mum and Dad, the love of my wife Ruth
and the joy of Clive, Kate, Emily, Scott, Jamie and Daniel

Contents

INTRODUCTION

I am writing my memoirs, because friends and family suggested that I capture my true life stories for others to share. That sits comfortably with a basic need of mine to get my experiences and feelings down on paper. I want to express my happiness with my life and explain to you how this came about. I also hope that my children and grandchildren will read about the way our family has developed and what kind of legacy we each leave for the next generation. It helps that I have written a diary entry every day from the age of ten!

So, if I am literally as happy as Larry, what leads to happiness? Can a family build a tradition of certain behaviours that will continue to bring personal joy? My parents both loved me and gave me good advice, so that was an excellent start in life.

A legacy which embraces happiness is partly inherited and partly what you create yourself. We must try to build on the good we have received, act as role models and, when permitted, be advisors to others. So, what would be my advice to the next generations?

Well, who would want my advice anyway? You might say that if we took our parents' or grandparents' advice, our way of life would never change and the world would never advance. Nonetheless, I will offer you some ideas covering what I have been fortunate to learn over the years, as well as experiences that have brought me personal satisfaction and at times much joy. Writing this book has been hard work and a great pleasure.

I know that our family legacy will be built on love and giving, as well as the pursuit of happiness.

Larry Brooks 2010

-1-

A VERY HUMBLE START

'All the world's a stage and all the men and women merely players'
(As You Like It by William Shakespeare, 1600)

Mum, Dad and baby Gordon moved from Leyton, east London, to rent the upstairs floor of an end-of-terrace house in Muswell Hill, north London in 1940. My elder sister Colleen and I were born in the front bedroom overlooking the narrow street. I arrived in March 1947, following a dreadfully cold winter. This meant that Mum had to carry me throughout those freezing conditions and often climb that tall, narrow staircase to our rooms.

Eighteen months before I was born, my parents, Joseph and Lilian, lost a baby girl, Pauline, to pneumonia. She was just three months old. Losing a child is deeply sad and, I am sorry to say, was rather common in those days. A generation earlier, my maternal grandmother, born Edith Dyer, was one of seventeen children, nine of whom died in the poverty and squalor of east London.

When Mum was pregnant with me, Colleen wanted a little sister and decorated the crib with pretty pink material. Mum would change it to blue, as she was sure it was to be a boy, so Colleen would change it back to pink. Colleen was not disappointed for long, as she informed me a little while ago that I was a lovely little boy with a heart full of love. It was kind of her to tell me that.

As Mum also had my eight-year-old brother and five-year-old sister to care for, it was clear that she never had it easy. Her washing, for example, had to be passed through a mangle to remove most of the water, and then pegged on to a line accessible only via a pulley from the upstairs window. Many of us will remember the mangle with its big handle and pair of rollers to squeeze the water out of the family washing. I once read that in 1951 there was a survey of how London housewives spent their time. It found that they worked an average of fifteen hours per day, chiefly preparing meals, washing clothes and cleaning the house. Most of the women shopped on Fridays, spending between ten shillings (50p) and two pounds. In 2010 this would equate to between twelve pounds and fifty pounds.

The lady downstairs was a nurse who received and treated wounded World War II soldiers in her own home. In 1952, she moved away and Dad took the opportunity to transfer his growing family to the ground floor. There, for the first time, we had a long, leafy garden that disappeared into overhanging lilac trees. The only downside of this exciting move was that we no longer had a bathroom, so it was a grey, metal tub in front of the lounge fire for bath night each Friday and a separate loo next to the small kitchen. Going to the toilet was rather cold in the winter, so we also had the traditional pot under the bed. My younger sister Marilyn (named after Miss Monroe) was born in the front room downstairs, when I was five. This meant that the pecking order for the one tub of hot water was Marilyn, me, Colleen and finally Gordon. My brother was now aged fifteen and had started work, so he had his turn with some privacy, once we had all gone to bed!

In that garden, Dad indulged in his hobby of breeding budgerigars, which he exhibited at shows. He became very good at this and started to win major championships. He built one large aviary in the middle of the garden and several smaller ones with sleeping quarters and breeding facilities against the wooden fences. As we were quite poor, he had to acquire his materials for the sheds and aviaries with remarkable skill and at little cost. He also applied this aptitude to obtaining good quality budgerigars, thought by their owners to be past their best, and he successfully bred many prize-winning, top class birds. We loved pets and were very fortunate to have two tortoises, named Saffy & Waffy, which Dad said all pets should be called! He assured me that Saffy was a boy's name and Waffy was that of a girl. Tortoises were inexpensive and readily available in those days. They had their names on their shells in white enamel paint in case they got lost, as they wandered freely around the lawn and pretty borders. I remember, as a little lad, feeding a long green dandelion leaf into the hungry gape of one of these characters, when something distracted me. I was brought back with a jolt when I found the tortoise biting my thumb. It left an interesting semi-circular red mark, which I mused over for some time. We had them toddling around the garden for many years and they successfully hibernated in late autumn in an old straw-lined wooden box in a little shed. That was until one freezing winter when they died of the cold along with the vast majority of all British tortoises. I was quite shocked when I peered into their box and found that they would not wake up. This was a great shame for such super little pets.

We also had several guinea pigs, all called Saffy and Waffy I expect. They were housed in an old converted kitchen cupboard, which stood in the narrow, stone yard. They were friendly, furry little pets and we would play with them on the small neat lawn outside our lounge window. Around the borders of the garden we could find a number of brown warty toads and I would feed them small worms. I watched their eyes moving around, studying the food offering until they suddenly opened their wide mouths and snatched their prey. I wanted some frogs, but you did not see them in that part of north London in those days. Sometimes, I would wander to a local, mucky stream, where I enjoyed collecting little fish like sticklebacks. I managed to keep them quite happily in a large old tank of rainwater in a corner of the garden. In our bedroom we had a metal cage with narrow bars that was full of fancy pet mice, but there were also grey house mice under our beds, playing around most nights. I remember hearing them knock my stray marbles around the lino. The sound of their little scratchy feet was quite distinctive, followed by the rolling of a marble until it knocked gently against the wooden skirting board. We did not have a cat to deter them in case it also worried Dad's budgies.

I learned to love birds, animals and nature in my early years and still do to this day. I also learned not to harm other living creatures and to respect life, all of which made me a happy and contented little lad.

Our family sleeping arrangements were probably not uncommon in those days. Mum and Dad's bedroom was what would normally be the downstairs 'front room'. My elder brother Gordon slept on the settee in the living room, once we had vacated it for the evening. I shared a bed with the girls, while we were still quite small. Two of us slept at one end of the bed and one of us at the other. It was quite good fun and fairly warm, considering there was very little heating in the house. Mum knitted us essential bed socks from old, unpicked woollen garments. They were the socks of many colours, just like my short-sleeved pullovers. The evening fire in the living room was put out as soon as we all went to bed in order to save coal. Prior to that we would huddle around it, sometimes wearing outdoor coats, like a scene from a Dickens novel.

When I was four years old, I spent my first and, so far, only night in hospital due to tonsillitis. I cannot remember anything in my life before that, but I have three specific memories of that occasion. Following the removal of my tonsils, I experienced the sheer joy of ice cream for the first time. This was to cool my sore throat and it was wonderful. A bit like your first incredulous experience of snow! Also, I clearly remember a quiet little boy named Charlie in the next bed. He was thin, pale and bald. My parents looked at him and glanced sadly at one another. Although I was only four, I could tell something was seriously wrong. The third thing I recollect was being brought home to find that Dad had produced our first television. This was supposedly to celebrate my homecoming, but Mum said it was for Dad to watch sport. There was only one channel, the BBC. I do not know how Dad managed to get a television, as we had no money, but it was certainly not stolen. In fact, there were only 350,000 televisions in Britain, despite a population of fifty million people, mostly because the only transmitter was in the London area.

Two years later, in 1953, neighbours came in to watch the tiny black and white screen for the broadcast of the Queen's coronation. As televisions were not that common, I remember thinking that it was strange to see a group of people all staring in one direction at a little fuzzy moving image on a box in the corner. Little did I know of what was to come from this medium!

My dad was always known as Joe. He had been a bright student, but his education was ended by the need to earn money to help support his parents and younger siblings. At first he became a bus conductor, then, because it paid more, a bus driver. This involved taking part of the bus driving test on the skid patch to learn how to handle the vehicle in slippery conditions. It also meant working shifts, which Dad assured me led to poor eating and sleeping patterns. In his case, this in turn led to painful indigestion and gall bladder problems. One of Dad's tips for me was not to work shifts and, as he died in 1976 following an operation to remove his gall bladder, I bore that advice in mind. Dad was five feet seven and a half inches tall, which he pointed out was the average height for a man, in case I thought he was short. He weighed nine stone seven pounds for most of his adult life and seemed fairly fit to me. For example, he would happily run around the local park kicking a football with Gordon and me. His dark brown hair always appeared black due to the regular application of Brylcreem. His eyes were blue and he nearly always had a healthy complexion and broad smile. He was rather handsome as a young man, in the mould of Errol Flynn, the Hollywood actor, as he briefly sported a small thin moustache.

Dad's father, another Joseph Brooks of similar appearance, was a furniture dealer with a shop in Bethnal Green. He also sold prams and Dad would do some deliveries for him around the local, narrow streets by handcart. The family shop took a direct hit in the wartime Blitz of 1941 and was destroyed. A rather bland block of flats now stands where the shop once stood. I believe that their premises were not insured, so my grandparents moved in with my Dad's two younger brothers and their wives, just four doors away from our house in Muswell Hill. My uncle Len's two daughters were born there, so it must have been quite crowded at times.

Mum was a milliner before marriage and motherhood. The hat shop, owned by a Mrs Goldstein, was in Roman Road, Bethnal Green, and Mum would be despatched to the West End to note down and copy the elaborate and exotic ladies' hats in the best shops. The fancy hats Mum made were displayed for sale in Roman Road and she would often be rewarded with Mrs G's cast off, top quality clothes. Mum was five feet five inches tall and of slim build with jet black hair. She looked very attractive in the boss's hats and fur coats and I have the photographs to prove it. Her maiden name was Harvey and she was not unlike a Hollywood actress of that period, also called Lilian Harvey and born in London. I guess I got my black hair from Mum, but at five feet ten and a half, I grew to be some inches taller than any of my immediate ancestors, so that's a mystery. Apart from my black hair, my distinguishing features, as a little lad, included a fairly large round head, big ears, freckles and missing teeth. As I wore short grey trousers until I was thirteen and was constantly rolling around the ground, my knees were always grazed with ugly marks. I suppose I was a bit scruffy.

By the way, my grandchildren are delighted to point out that my hair is no longer black, but I have not told them that I am barely five feet ten now! Although my son and I are the same height, my nephew, another Joseph Brooks, is an amazing six feet two. More about these folk later.

Gordon was born in a rented terraced house in Leyton in 1938 and Mum vividly recalled pushing his pram through the local park and seeing the frightening doodlebugs whiz over her head during the war. The doodlebug was the name given to the V-1 flying bomb. The 'V' stood for Vergeltungswaffe, which was German for 'vengeance weapon'. Mum also remembered the dreadful sight of houses destroyed by bombs in Bethnal Green, very close to her own family's homes, and worrying enormously as to whether any of her relatives had been hit. Fortunately, she was evacuated to Hertfordshire with baby Gordon, who tells me that he lost his teddy bear on the train. There were still bomb sites with craters and remains of fallen houses in east London, when I visited Petticoat Lane and Club Row markets with my Dad in the late 1950's.

My Mum's father, John Harvey, was a GPO foreman and Mum proudly recounted to me that he had been a mounted rifleman in the Hussars. She said he was five feet seven inches tall with grey eyes and always sported a small moustache. Very recently, I went to the National Archives at Kew and discovered that he was in the 11th Hussars for twelve years, including serving in the Boer War and at the Relief of Ladysmith. He later served in World War One from 1914 to 1919, so I think he did his bit. He told Mum that he often had pals killed around him in battle and was lucky to survive seventeen years of very active service. Remarkable.

During World War Two, Dad was a Leading Aircraftsman in the RAF and was based at various airfields in southern England. He was given extensive training as an aircraft mechanic in order to repair planes damaged in the conflict. Dad left Britain only once in his life and even then his feet did not touch foreign soil. He was flown over France and possibly Germany, as ground staff had to take a trip in the planes they were responsible for repairing. This brought home to them the importance of their jobs. Dad recalled that the worst part of his job, apart from running for cover during air raids, was helping injured airmen from the damaged planes. Many a rear gunner was no longer alive when removed from the aircraft. Dad did not like to see a fellow serviceman or any living creature in pain and I feel sad that he and countless others had to experience the horrors of war. Whilst in the RAF, a landlady of his once came to him with her badly injured cat, run over by a car, and a large hammer asking him to put the cat out of its misery! She was both distraught and certain that he must kill it. Dad, with great reluctance, did his duty, having first covered the poor creature's head with a cloth.

Coincidentally, as I write this chapter in July 2009, I have just learnt of the death of the greatest air mechanic of the First World War and, at one hundred and thirteen years, the world's oldest man, Henry Allingham.

He was a remarkable man and I am pleased that Dad shared that wartime occupation with him. Henry lived long enough to see his first great-great-great-grandchild, which I think I will make an ambition of mine too!

On the brighter side, Dad played football in the RAF with Stan Mortensen, who was a Blackpool and England colleague of the legendary Stanley Matthews. Mortensen was the only player to score a hat-trick in a Wembley Cup Final and the first to score for England in a FIFA World Cup qualifying campaign. He was a wireless operator and the only survivor when his bomber crashed. Playing with Stan pleased Dad, as he was a football fan and a lifelong supporter of Tottenham Hotspur FC, as was his father. He later made sure that his children supported 'Spurs' and that's another legacy that continues to my children and grandsons. Thanks for putting even more pleasure my way, Dad.

I did see Stanley Matthews play top flight football at Spurs when he was fifty-two years old. He was on the right wing, as usual, and up against our very good left-back, Cyril Knowles. I got the distinct impression that young Cyril was wary of him and either did not want to be beaten by Stan or did not want to be the guy who went in hard and hurt him. Nonetheless Stan had quite a good game.

In January 2009, I began to wonder whether Dad had earned any war medals, because I had never seen any. I wrote, more in hope than expectation, to the MOD Medal Office in Gloucester and they sent me two gleaming medals in mint condition. I guess that Dad had either not bothered or could not afford to collect them at the time. Still, I am very pleased to have them.

Oh, by the way, I was baptised Laurence Brooks, but always called Larry. The idea for the name came from an American called Larry that Dad met in the RAF. Dad also liked the popular and handsome British actor Laurence Olivier, also known as Larry, so maybe that clinched it.

Back to my first family home, number two Goodwyns Vale, Muswell Hill. Colleen was born during the war in 1941. She told me that when money was tight, Mum would go without food in order to feed the children, but without necessarily telling Dad. I do not remember this phase, but I do know that I have always been grateful for my meals and always cleared my plate. Colleen particularly recalls a time that Dad came home and found the children hungry. 'Lil!' he shouted. 'What's going on?' When he realised that there was no food in the house, he raced up the road to his parents for eggs, bread and milk. Post-war food rationing did not help anybody's situation and I once read that in the year of my birth, 1947, there were one thousand people in a queue for bread at a London shop.

When I was eight years old, my pocket money rose from three pence to six pence per week, which I had to earn by helping Dad with his budgerigars. The increase allowed me to buy a halfpennyworth of broken sweets from the big jars in the shop window, when sweet-rationing ended in 1954. I could also afford a weekly comic, the Beano, which I found very amusing. I had to walk a mile up to Muswell Hill Broadway for this on a Sunday morning after attending the Cub Scouts. I would start reading it absent-mindedly on the way back downhill to my home. Colleen says I was always reading something! Another important job I had was to be first outside with a bucket and shovel, when the milkman's big brown horse delivered some manure for our garden. My little legs moved very quickly and I was never beaten. This valuable treasure was either left to rot in a smelly heap or liquidised in an old barrel by Gordon and Dad, who used it as the only form of fertiliser in our garden. Just like most men I knew, Dad grew some vegetables for the dinner table. I seem to remember eating quite a lot of stew with carrots and potatoes and I do not recollect ever being really hungry. Dad always praised my efforts with the bucket, so I felt quite pleased with myself.

As head of the household, Dad had a special chair that only he used. It was old and brown with thin wooden arms and it reclined a little, so that he could nod off occasionally after a hard day's work. I clearly remember the pleasure of sitting on his lap in that chair for my evening cuddle. I would rub his chin, which by bedtime was rather rough with bristly hair breaking through. He would gently stroke my smooth face and chant 'Smoothy'. When it was little Marilyn's turn for five minutes in his 'parlour', he repeated 'Fives' as she also got this early form of facial massage. Many apparently sensible dads invented funny little sayings under the influence of children.

Goodwyns Vale seemed large and wide, when I was small, probably because nobody had a car to clutter the road. When I returned as an adult, I realised how small and cramped the street really was. Among my friends were two Indian children, whose father was a doctor. I occasionally went to play in their house and was treated very well. I noticed that they had plenty of food and sweets. I knew not to ask for such things, but they were generous and I do remember little occasions like tasting my first Polo mint.

I managed to make some extra money by collecting, sorting and returning various glass bottles to shops, which paid a bounty on each one. This enabled me to buy some plastic Airfix kits of Spitfires and Messerschmits to hang from my bedroom ceiling and re-enact the air battles of the war. My later Airfix kits were all British birds, as my interests turned towards nature. Another small source of income was taking old newspapers to the fish and chip shops. After wrapping the food in some new, white paper, they would wrap the whole thing in newspaper to keep it warm on your way home. It would be called recycling nowadays, but shops no longer take your old papers. It's probably due to 'health and safety'.

Apart from a garden full of pets, a memorable feature of our stay downstairs was the coal bunker under the stairs. It served as a dark, somewhat scary hiding place and I am not sure that we ever had much coal in it. I think we could only afford to buy fuel in small amounts, so it was often kept beside the fire in a metal bucket.

The foot of the stairs served as our first-floor neighbours' entrance to their accommodation. They would enter the communal door from the street and walk past Mum and Dad's bedroom, before going upstairs. There was no locked door to separate them from us. They were a quiet, pleasant young couple, but I do not remember seeing them very often, despite the fact that they must have spent a little time in our passageway each morning and evening.

Mum had to go out to work, mostly serving in nearby shops, in order to help make ends meet. It was no mean task for her to bring up four children and support Dad. Her outlet was an occasional trip to the pictures with her friend 'Ginger Lil from Muswell Hill'. She liked to see the dashingly good-looking American film stars like Errol Flynn and Douglas Fairbanks, Junior. She was quite a romantic really and enjoyed reading love stories, in particular the popular Mills and Boon novels.

Dad made some extra cash at the weekends by making nesting boxes for budgies. In the evenings he would sit at the dining table carefully constructing crystal set radios from soap dishes and bought-in components. He sold all these items either privately or to Club Row market traders in east London. We would take trips there on Sunday mornings and Dad would buy me a slice of bread and dripping, which I thoroughly enjoyed at the time. Eating bread and animal fat has lost its appeal nowadays. I recall sitting next to a very old, shabbily dressed Indian man in our favourite cafe. Dad bought him a cup of tea and gave him sixpence, because he felt sorry for him.

As we had little money, Christmas was always an exciting time. It sounds like a cliché, but it was the only occasion that we had a chicken for dinner, a bottle of fizzy pop and an orange. My best present was a toy, double-barrelled shotgun that fired two corks, which could not go far as each was attached to the gun by string. Naturally, being a boy, I removed the pieces of string. I did manage to accumulate a large number of toy soldiers and, like most boys, enjoyed playing with them enormously. I also liked painting groups of them, as if they were wearing special uniforms, so that they could fight little battles.

Dad left the buses and joined the BBC as a wages clerk, first at the great Alexandra Palace, known affectionately as Ally Pally, and later at Broadcasting House in Portland Place, London. He would often tell us of the television stars he met, including the very friendly and funny characters like Harry Secombe and Arthur Askey. Like me, he preferred genuine, down-to-earth folk, whatever their position, and disliked any form of snobbery or pretentiousness.

I do not think Dad missed a day's work, as he thought that it was his duty to be there at all costs. After all, they were paying his wages. During a bus strike lasting several days, he would walk to central London and back, approximately six miles each way. He left home very early to make sure that he was not late. He soon acquired a rather large old green bicycle and started cycling to work. Finally, he turned the bike into a moped or 'pop-pop' by fitting an equally ancient motor to the rear wheel. Dad also acquired a helmet to protect his head. They were not a legal requirement, but he thought it was a sensible idea. Our neighbours had a motorbike with a sidecar attached and the chap would drive while his wife sat in this rickety wooden contraption beside him. Neither wore a helmet.

Every summer, Dad managed to take us on a little holiday to Southend by train. The compartments were separate and Dad wanted the six of us to have one to ourselves, although there was room for about two more people. At each station en route to our destination, he encouraged us four children to leap around the windows like maniacs to repel boarders. I do not think anybody ever got in the train compartment with us. Rest assured that there was plenty of room along the train otherwise Dad would not have let us do it.

We always stayed for about a week at the same bed and breakfast close to the beach and spent most of the time playing on the sand. Dad was the only swimmer in our family and would trawl up and down for a while, quite some distance from shore. He stopped that activity after getting cramp and only just making it back to land without drowning. After that he was content to place a knotted hankie on his head, roll up his trouser legs and have a paddle. I remember holding his hand as he coaxed me into getting my feet wet for the first time. I held tight as the cold sea water and sand trickled between my toes.

My brother and I had woollen, yes woollen, swimming trunks, knitted by Mum from recycled jumpers. It is a lasting memory seeing Gordon walk up the beach with greenish-brown sodden shorts hanging round his knees.

We took two friends, a lady and her daughter, to Southend with us one year. All I can remember is Dad telling me some years later that the lass, who had liked dancing, became a Tiller Girl. These were a chorus line of high-kicking, synchronised dancers, who linked arms until they had to turn around, when they briefly separated. They were all the same height and build, so the routines were completely uniform and precise. They famously appeared on television in Sunday Night at the London Palladium, which was initially hosted by the most popular Tommy Trinder. Every year we would ask Dad what he wanted for Christmas and he would reply 'One of the Tiller Girls'.

I am often intrigued by the kinds of minor incidents that one remembers. I was holding Dad's hand as we entered an amusement arcade in Southend, but let go for a moment to scratch my leg. When I grabbed his hand again, I looked up to find a complete stranger grinning at me from above. Shocked, I turned round to find Dad smiling too. I have occasionally noticed other children make that innocent little mistake. Bless.

So far in my life, my increasing happiness was due to loving parents, who gave us their precious time, a brother and sisters who were kind to me and a variety of pets!

-2-

SCHOOL IN NORTH LONDON

'Education is not preparation for life; education is life itself.'
(John Dewey, 1900)

My first primary school, in Muswell Hill, was a mile walk uphill, crossing the busy Colney Hatch Lane. On one occasion, when I was ten years old, a big red double-decker bus missed me by inches as I thoughtlessly dashed across the road in front of it. I did not dare tell Mum how stupid I had been, but a neighbour, known to all as Nosey Parker, spotted the incident and informed her that evening. Mum had a serious word with me. I believe I am fortunate that my parents never once hit me or not that I can remember. I suppose it is a consequence that I have yet to strike another person. I hope that I never have cause.

I enjoyed learning and did not miss a single day's schooling. Even when I sprained my foot and walked with a painful limp, there was no question of my being allowed to stay at home. Dad and Mum both worked all day to pay the rent and feed four hungry children, so my elder sister Colleen had to support me and my bad foot all the way to school. In any event, I did not want to miss any lessons, as it I knew it was important. By the way, schools did not close when it snowed in those days. Also, hardly anyone, including us, had a car to try and drive in icy conditions, so we just had to overcome such problems and get around as best as we could.

I believe that my determination to get to school led to my later work ethic, missing only four and a half days through illness in nearly forty years. This was due to some luck and sheer bloody-mindedness. If you are of an inquisitive nature, I was off sick from work for a day on two separate occasions with gastro enteritis, during which I could hardly stand, and two and a half days with a flu-type virus, which laid out better men than me for two to four weeks.

When I was ten and a half, we moved from Muswell Hill to Edmonton, also in north London, to buy our own house. This meant that we had an entire, three bedroom terraced house to ourselves, as well as a back garden. Mum was very pleased to have a bathroom again and would show it to visitors! Dad was taking out his first mortgage at the age of forty-seven. I remember him telling me that it was a twenty-five year mortgage, so he would, theoretically be seventy-two when he paid it off. He actually repaid it in eight years, as he soon changed his job to become an insurance agent and was very successful. Mum and Dad had the main bedroom, my sisters shared the next largest room and I was on a bunk bed above Gordon in the tiny box-room overlooking the street. Once again, Dad developed breeding facilities for his budgies at the end of the garden. It was around that time that I reported to Dad that I had seen a woman, yes a woman, driving a car. He smiled at this and I realised that it was probably a bit more common than I thought, but I did not know any ladies who could drive.

My new school, Houndsfield primary, which I would attend for less than a year, had a famous old boy. He was the England and Fulham striker Johnny Haynes. Apart from being a very good player, he hit the headlines for being the first footballer to earn £100 per week in 1961. The maximum weekly wage of £20 had not long been abolished. As we know, the wages floodgates were subsequently flung wide open. Anyway, the main point is that I switched schools just before I had to take the famous eleven plus examination, which determined whether or not I would attend a grammar school or secondary modern. Several counties still have the eleven plus, including Kent, where my eldest grandchildren passed the test in the years 2006 and 2009.

I did pass and in September 1958 went to the school that Dad selected as first choice, Enfield Grammar School for Boys. The school was founded in 1557 and had an excellent academic record, so Dad thought it would be a good, prestigious education for me. In 1976 I found a hand-written draft of the letter Dad wrote to the BBC Benevolent Fund, when he was still a clerk at Broadcasting House. He basically pointed out that his son Laurence had passed the eleven plus and the complete uniform would cost eleven pounds and fifteen shillings, whereas he only earned ten pounds, three shillings and sixpence a week. He carefully itemised how his wages were spent, including rent, food, clothing, utilities and general household needs. It left very little for the kinds of things we try to budget for nowadays, like entertainment or foreign holidays. Dad had a very pleasant reply from the chairman of the fund, granting him the money for my uniform and wishing me well for the future. Dad actually left the BBC fairly soon after this event, but I have always had a warm feeling towards the corporation.

My new school was three and a half miles from home and required two bus journeys each way. In the great London smogs, caused by fog and air pollution, visibility was almost zero and the buses did not run, so I had to walk from home to school and back. I bumped into some lampposts and walls in those days and tripped up some kerbs. There were still a few vehicles moving in the smog, so you had to avoid those too. It was a bit tough for a little boy of eleven with compulsory short trousers and cold legs. The word 'smog' was derived from the two words 'smoke' and 'fog'. Luckily the new Clean Air Act only allowed the burning of smokeless fuels and smog became a thing of the past, as did that nasty taste of sulphur in the air.

One of the pleasures of starting secondary school and Dad earning more money was that he no longer cut my hair with scissors and a pudding basin over the top of my head. He tried dog clippers for a while, but now I was actually given money for the barbers. Once I went to a new hairdressers and he used the recently-developed electric clippers, which I thought was amazing. I declared to him, in front of other customers, that it was the best haircut that I had ever had. Nowadays, I always have my hair cut at home by my wife Ruth, but more of her later.

A regular activity of mine was writing to my brother who was one of the last young men to be conscripted into the army to do his 'national service'. I enjoyed addressing the envelopes to 'gunner' or 'sapper' and I can recite his eight digit service number to this day. I would tell him all our news at home to try to keep him cheerful, as he did not really enjoy the whole experience.

Early in my grammar school career, I took home a note from the French master. It was about a school trip to France costing £30 for two weeks. As I had never been further than Southend for our little annual summer break, it seemed a marvellous, but out of reach opportunity. I thought I was wasting my time and I felt guilty about the huge cost when I handed it to Dad, but after a while he said, 'Yes'. Thinking back, there was no jealousy from my older brother and sister, who, like Mum and Dad, had never had this chance in life. Dad saved every penny he could to get the deposit and eventual balance for the trip. I expect we all went without and I know that Dad existed on just one or two cigarettes a day. During that period, I rarely went to the tobacconist for an ounce of Golden Virginia or Old Holborn tobacco and Dad's half-pint of prawns for his Sunday treat went by the wayside for a while too. He tried really hard to give me some opportunities and that makes me feel very good. Incidentally, that love of prawns has been passed to every subsequent generation, including my granddaughter Emily, but more of her later.

On the day of the school trip, I had to meet the group at Victoria station. Dad had upgraded from his motorised bicycle to a brand new Vespa scooter to go with his new job, so he took me into London on the pillion. I was wearing my school uniform of navy blue jacket and short grey trousers, as they were my best clothes. As I sat behind Dad, holding onto him for dear life with one hand and clutching my little brown suitcase in the other, I was a bit concerned when we were stopped by a policeman. He told Dad that my feet were protruding from the sides of the scooter and I could break an ankle when we cornered. Dad thanked him and got me safely to the meeting point.

The trip to Grenoble in the French Alps was via Paris. The whole experience was brilliant and really broadened my horizons. I borrowed a little Kodak Brownie camera and took some really good photos from the top of the Eiffel Tower. I still love the Eiffel Tower.

A strange, lasting memory for me in Grenoble was an extremely strong sand storm, during which I saw a bicycle and a ladder moving vertically along the street unaided by man. We had been for a walk, but were now pinned in doorways until the storm subsided, by which time we had sand in every orifice.

The stay in Grenoble included a visit to a monastery inhabited by Carthusian monks of the Chartreuse order. The monks had taken a vow of silence and we boys were all very surprised by this. Just as surprising to me was that these sombre, holy men in their plain brown habits produced and sold alcohol. Somehow I had enough spending money to buy a small bottle of Chartreuse liqueur for Dad and I remember how his eyes lit up when he saw it. One of our male teachers had drunk one of these and fallen flat on his back, so I warned Dad when I got home. I also managed to buy a little doll in costume for Marilyn and something for Mum. Dad eked out his present over a few days, so he did not suffer the same fate as my schoolmaster!

Dad's new Vespa rather let him down one day. Whilst riding in front of a bus, the handlebars came off. He said he threw his body into the gutter and rolled onto the pavement, whilst the bus missed him by inches. His replacement scooter was a Lambretta. Dad was a careful driver, but having just travelled over a hump-back bridge he hit a spill of gravel the other side and came off the machine. Now fed up with being on two wheels, it was not long before he bought a three-wheeler Reliant van, as used by Del Boy in Only Fools and Horses. The main thing was that it was warm and dry and Mum was thrilled to be driven around rather than walk everywhere. She would rarely spend precious money on bus fares unless she was going a very long distance. Dad could also take a large number of budgies to bird shows in the van. Each of our feathered friends had a scrupulously clean individual cage, carefully packed into the back of the vehicle and we would go to shows in such exotic places as sunny Ramsgate in Kent!

Having been top in every subject at primary school, it was a bit of a shock mixing with such really academic boys at the grammar school and I was very pleased to get into the top set for each subject. It interests me the way that a child's choice of subjects has improved over the years. At the age of thirteen, I had to choose between 'arts' and 'science'. As I wanted to take O levels in biology and physics, I also had to study chemistry, but give up history, geography and Spanish. We all took English language, English literature, mathematics, additional mathematics, Latin and French. I achieved the expected nine O levels and advanced to the sixth form, where I went on to take pure maths, applied maths and physics at A level. I did take A level general maths a year early, aged seventeen, simply as practice, and was quite satisfied with a grade C.

The really clever lads also took A level chemistry plus a couple of spare O levels like music and religious instruction. The standard was so high that ten boys went on to Oxford and Cambridge Universities, which was expected of our school with its four hundred years of tradition. Despite passing an Oxbridge entrance exam, my two grade B's and a C hardly matched the three or four grade A's achieved by the geniuses, so it would be a lesser university for me and even more mathematics to study. Still, I had exceeded expectations and Mum and Dad were thrilled for me. I would overhear them proudly telling people that their son was 'at grammar school'.

Back to my first day at Enfield Grammar, which found me seated next to a fellow Spurs supporter named Bob. Whereas my father had been unable to afford to take me to see them play, this lad had been to many games and really knew his stuff. I discovered more recently that he eventually became Solicitor General of Hong Kong, but have unfortunately lost touch with him. His first act at school was to make me learn the names of the Spurs team, which I remember to this day, then he would test me till I got it right. He also persuaded me to ask Dad if I could go to Spurs with him. Dad agreed and I must say that there was little better in football than watching Spurs in the early 1960s. Each home game would cost a shilling, which was twelve old pence or five new pence nowadays. I sound really old, don't I, but I certainly don't feel it. The twelve pence broke down as follows: two pence each way on the bus from Edmonton to Tottenham, two pence for a programme and sixpence to get in the boys' entrance. It's gone up a bit since then! We rarely missed a home game during a great spell for the Spurs, including the 1961 league and cup double.

An outstanding memory of the grammar school was the extraordinary behaviour of a boy known as Monkey. His imaginative antics became my grandchildren's favourite stories. He played many unusual tricks on teachers, but his piece de resistance involved a tall blackboard that revolved around two horizontal spindles. A teacher could write on a panel using chalk, then move it up or down and write on the next panel and so on. The panels would disappear to the back and reappear as the next one was pushed up or down, like a vertical conveyor belt. It meant that you could retain information and bring it back for further discussion, before wiping it clean with a board rubber.

Monkey thought it would be fun to write a simple message like 'BOO!' on the board and push the panel over the top, so that it would hopefully appear during a lesson. More than that, Monkey, a skinny lad, found that he was able to squeeze under the board and hide behind it, which is where he was when the maths teacher came in. If he had noticed Monkey's empty chair, it would have been with pleasure, poor man, as he had no time for this particularly mischievous pupil. The teacher was a large, sinister-looking man known as 'Crippen' after the murderer Dr Crippen, because he had a similar name. His behaviour was rather strange and I believe that he could have a book on psychiatry devoted entirely to him. He would tell us things like the world would be ended by a giant flood on Friday and he would not be at school that day. It seems that he spent that occasion at the top of a mountain in France. He was also one of those teachers who threw pieces of chalk and board rubbers at boys who were misbehaving. This could be very painful for those he managed to hit. I assure you that he was unbalanced before he met Monkey, but he was finally tipped over the edge by the boy.

One unsuspecting day, Crippen had decided to teach us how to calculate the angles of a triangle using the lengths of the three sides. He drew a triangle with sides 13, 5 and 11 inches long, but before we could copy this into our books, he moved the panel up to check that all the other boards were clean. He found 'BOO!' of course and gave us a horrid, twisted little smile. It was more of a sneer really. He erased the unwanted word and retrieved his triangle drawing from round the back. He had not noticed that Monkey had changed the number representing the length of one side from 11 to 7. Although his drawing was untouched and still looked OK, the triangle was now impossible with sides 13, 5 and 7. If you try drawing it accurately, you will find it does not exist. We all copied the triangle and used Crippen's formula to find the three angles. None of us could get any sensible results, so he decided to show us how to do it. He became very frustrated as nothing would go right. He checked his original notes, looked at the triangle and realised the mistake, which he thought was down to him. Then he pulled the board down and found another 'BOO!' At that point he twigged that this was happening in real time and somebody was behind the board. I have rarely seen such fury. He managed to pull Monkey out by the feet and twisting his arm, pinned him to a desk and shook him hard. He then dragged him to the headmaster's office, which was Monkey's second home.

When we next had maths, Crippen noticed that Monkey's chair was empty, so he decided to look under the revolving blackboard. What he did not know was that Monkey was hiding under his desk and had left a pair of shoes under the blackboard. Crippen shrieked with rage and grabbed these 'feet'. When they came straight out in his hands, he threw them around in anger and dived under the board looking for Monkey, who by this time was calmly seated at his desk. He had actually done little wrong this time, but Crippen was incensed and tried a fumbled attack on the lad, before recoiling to his chair, mentally and physically drained. Although the class fell about laughing at these high jinks, I saw another side to this fiasco. I remember feeling that there was something rather disturbing about the behaviour of both of them, as well as the fact that we were missing some important maths. I dwelt on this for a while, but had no solution (pun).

As I walked to the bus stop later that day, our illustrious maths teacher was walking ahead of me. I must have glanced away, then looked back and he had mysteriously disappeared. As I passed a shop, he was pinned in the door way calling out, 'Stop following me.' I was surprised at the outburst, but sadly shook my head and felt quite sorry for him.

We had a very unpleasant young teacher known as Herr Weber, who was quite keen on physical violence in the days that teachers could get away with it, if they wished. He quite liked hitting you as hard as possible across the hand with a wooden ruler for the slightest reason. He even entered the classroom one day and struck everyone on the palm 'as a warning'. It was very painful, but we had to put up with it. I have never liked being punished unfairly.

Conversely, a very sweet, little old lady taught us English. She was as bright as a button and she absolutely adored poetry. Among other classics, she coaxed us to learn 'Composed upon Westminster Bridge', a beautiful sonnet by William Wordsworth. The best of the rest were 'The Seven Ages of Man' from 'As You Like It' by William Shakespeare and Henry V's speech before Agincourt, beginning 'I am a king', again by Shakespeare. Our teacher assured us that one day we would be glad we had mastered such superb verse. I am indeed very pleased and can still recite them, with a little practice.

Everyone had school dinners in those days and they were usually very good, in my view. On one occasion, something possessed me to have salad, which the dinner lady handed over. As I moved along the line, I noticed a huge, red, gyrating worm emerge from under the lettuce and dance around my plate. I was so struck with horror that I just held out the plate and showed it to the lady. You may have guessed what she said, 'Would you like another one?' She meant salad, not worm, of course, but for probably the only time in my life, I did not fancy any food at all.

My sex education came from the biology mistress, as it did for most boys at our school. Her name was Fanny, which was not uncommon in those days, and she told us everything we needed to know. She left no stone unturned and some of her advice was very surprising, but all of it was useful. She was a sixty year old spinster, but 'by no means a virgin'. We would look suspiciously at the virile young male laboratory assistants that seemed to follow her around. She surprised us further by marrying the rather scary, aging deputy head, who sadly died shortly afterwards. You can imagine what we boys thought.

Our headmaster, a quiet, grey-haired, elderly chap, called a special assembly one morning. He informed the whole school that he had heard a word shouted in the playground and he never wanted to hear that word uttered again. He continued by informing us that he was about to say the word so that we would be perfectly clear what we were never to repeat. It was a bit worrying, as Lady Chatterley's Lover by D.H.Lawrence had just been released in Britain and everyone was becoming aware of 'that word'. However, the dear old head told us that the disgusting word that he had heard was 'clot'. He must be turning and turning in his grave at what we hear nowadays.

One day in July 1964, whilst walking between school buildings, I was caught in a sudden storm and had to dash for cover. There was thunder, lightning and torrential rain. I was soaked. Most sadly, I discovered that evening that a great Spurs favourite John White was also out that day and lost his life. The Scottish international footballer was sheltering under a tree at the nearby Crews Hill golf course, when it was struck by lightning and John was killed. He was a likeable, talented and creative midfielder, who was ever-present in the great league and cup double season of 1960/61, scoring thirteen goals. He won another FA Cup winner's medal during the next season and helped Spurs win the European Cup Winner's Cup in 1962/63. Ironically, John was known as The Ghost of White Hart Lane for his ability to appear out of nowhere to split a defence open with one incisive pass. John left a young widow and two small children, one of whom now has a daughter who, on a happier note, has been training at Spurs' ground in recent years.

After John's tragic death, I went to his testimonial match at White Hart Lane, where Spurs played a Scotland eleven. His brother played in John's position for Spurs and it was a good match, but I remember feeling rather sad at the reason for the game. However, I did like mixing with the Scottish supporters that had made the journey, as there was no separation of home and away fans. I enjoyed those days and can remember that there was good banter and no violence. In the league matches, I particularly liked the sense of humour of the Liverpool fans, one of whom caught me as I tripped and nearly fell off the terrace into a stair well. They were a very amusing bunch.

During my secondary school years, I built and maintained my interest in British birds, as well as my budgies. I joined the RSPB and went bird-watching with a friend, Alan, who first got involved when I pointed out a greenfinch in the school field. He went on to become chief engineer for a major British company. He wrote to me in 2007 thanking me for introducing him to nature and showing him what to do with the rest of his life! He has even written books on aspects of natural history, so that is good to know.

As a boy, I owned a bullfinch, which I assume had been taken from the wild. He had an exquisite red chest and shiny black cap and looked very smart. Finches were captured in huge numbers and were freely available for purchase in those days. I agree that, as with many other things, this is now totally wrong and unacceptable, but it was commonplace in the 1950s. I entered Bullie in pet shows and he always won a prize due to his beautiful condition and calm nature. He was very tame and would sit on my finger, accepting a small tit-bit of food from my other hand. He lived for several years and was my favourite pet of all time. One day in Club Row, east London, Dad bought me a pair of greenfinches for four shillings. He also gave me full use of an old wooden shed and I stuffed it with bushes, in which the greenies would breed. It seems odd to write about things that are now clearly wrong. Then again, dogs did their business on the pavement and drunks drove cars with bald tyres and it was all legal. Some things have improved a great deal over the years.

Club Row was a magnet for my brother and me. Gordon once persuaded Dad to let him buy two pretty little day-old chicks. Dad protested that the seller would know that they were young cockerels, as he would keep the hens for laying. Gordon won and looked after the chicks. They developed into the two most fabulous big Rhode Island Red chickens and laid around five eggs per week for several years. Dad loved them as much as we did and made sure that they were always looked after very well.

So, was that a happy period for me? Yes indeed. I was learning, I had great friends and family, I saw Spurs regularly and I had my pet birds, but before I left grammar school there was much more pleasure to come …

Gordon, Colleen, me and Marilyn in the garden in Muswell Hill, 1955

My mum, Lilian Harvey, aged 16

Dad, as I remember him

The Eiffel Tower and me, aged 12

-3-

IT'S WHO YOU KNOW

'Friendship is unnecessary, like philosophy, like art... It has no survival value; rather is one of those things that give value to survival.'
(C.S.Lewis, 1950)

It is said that it is often who you know that is more influential than what you know, so let me tell you a little about the budgerigar club, which Dad joined in 1952. Apart from giving us a great deal of pleasure, this was a hobby that changed our lives. Dad introduced Gordon and me to his new friends and to the art of breeding top class budgies, which we enjoyed for many years. It was also a lesson in how to achieve a goal. My brother went on to have high quality, valuable pigeons and all on a very tight budget. That's skill.

It was Dad's friends who altered the direction of our family and getting to know them opened my eyes to some intelligent, good-hearted men. They were prepared to help others for no financial reward, just friendship. The first budgie pal of great note was Fred Corney, a well-respected, senior manager for the Cooperative Insurance Society or CIS. At well over six feet, Fred was the tallest man I had met. He had a great sense of humour and seemed to like our family very much. He had a smart, detached house in Mill Hill, living amongst music impresarios and other wealthy types. Dad and I were guests at his house one day and we all decided to visit Fred's allotment, where he grew vegetables and roses. Before we left, he asked his gardener, a tubby little man, to creosote the fence. When we returned, the fence, the gardener and most of the pretty flowers were covered in the evil, smelly creosote. The chap chirpily asked, 'Have I missed anything?' Fred replied, 'There's a small patch of white skin behind your ear!'

Then it happened. Fred suggested that my Dad came to work for him as an insurance agent. This surprised me as I had not realised that people could change to a different type of job. Dad readily accepted Fred's offer and left the BBC immediately.

Within two years, Dad was the top-earning CIS agent in north London and had trebled his wages to more than £30 per week. He was so proud that he could not help but impart that information to me. I was only eleven, but I listened carefully and tried to understand the implications. I knew that if Dad told me something like that, he wanted me to understand and learn from it. He also pointed out that, when selling insurance and earning commission, the harder you worked, the more you earned. He had never been in that kind of occupation before. Like most employees, he was used to having a small rise once a year, if he was lucky. In 1963, having had two motor scooters and a van, he was able to buy his first car, a brand new Vauxhall Victor De Luxe! Mum felt like a queen. She had a house with a proper bathroom and was driven around in an elegant, new, gleaming white saloon car. Other men in our street would stop to admire the car and discuss its various attributes with Dad, who was just as pleased as Mum.

It was Fred who later kindly drove my future wife and me from north London to look at properties in Kent, as it would be easier by car and he had experience in house-buying matters. I remember my surprise when he chatted to potential neighbours about such things as what it was like to live in the area. He said that we should try to obtain a repayment mortgage via a building society, but if it was not granted, we should approach him regarding an endowment mortgage. He demonstrated real kindness and hands-on help, which was a wonderful lesson from a man I will never forget.

Going back to our first television in 1951, it was another budgie club pal who came to our house one day and fitted a switch onto the side of our set and, hey presto, a second channel called ITV!

Yet another good and useful friend at the club was George the butcher. He really looked the part thanks to his stocky build and ruddy complexion and he would always bring us a treat from his shop, when meat was very expensive. He introduced Mum to flaky pastry and she was really pleased with herself when she made her first delicious meat pie with this tasty topping. George came to our house one day and to my surprise he had a little black puppy nestling inside his shirt to keep warm. It wasn't food this time, it was a gift. It became Fred, the first of two poodles we would own. As a pup, Fred's hair was like the softest wool to touch and his breath had that pleasant and distinct smell unique to puppies. George also arrived on one occasion with a black spidery thing attached to his nose. I had never seen stitches before. He had braked suddenly in his car to avoid a dog and as there were no seat belts in those days, his face hit the windscreen. I secretly overheard him tell Dad that he wished he had hit the 'bloody thing'. Interestingly, our family did not really swear, but Dad would occasionally say 'bloody', as I remember.

Our second poodle was a white bitch called Freda. Not very imaginative, I know. When Fred got a bit too old, I would take Freda for her daily exercise in the park on her own. She was obsessed with chasing balls or sticks, which she did with great speed. She usually found her own sticks and all you had to do was throw it until you were too tired to continue. It was almost impossible to wear her out and she would dance around your feet until you threw it again. One day she presented me with a small, thin branch, which I threw instantly, because she also barked incessantly if you did not throw it. As it landed, one end stuck in some mud like a javelin and there was an even sharper end poking out. Freda was onto the protruding end of the stick at her usual high pace. Most unfortunately, it went right through her upper palate and she collapsed. I ran over and picked her up and there was blood everywhere. I pulled out the stick and carried her from the park, unsure whether she was dead or alive. I decided to get straight onto a bus to the vet's, but as I had no money, I gave the conductor my name and address and he allowed me to ride. Naturally, the other passengers stared at me sitting amongst them with the collapsed Freda on my lap. When I left the bus, I had to carry Freda some distance to the vet's. She was big and heavy for a poodle. The surgery was crowded, but I walked to the counter and the receptionist instantly called a vet. Although I was unable to pay, he gave Freda an injection and within a few minutes, she returned to consciousness and I could take her home. I believe she had fainted, but I do not know how I would have told Mum and Dad, if she had died. They loved Freda.

Anyway, please don't laugh at keeping budgies. In 1963, Dad sold a champion bird for £60, which was twice his weekly wage. However, he only sold it because he had several better birds, so he could continue breeding and exhibiting at top level and maintain his high status in the budgie world. I noticed that about twenty years later, the bird that won the Budgerigar National Exhibition was sold for £2000. Dad eventually sold all his budgies and his insurance round and bought a bungalow outright, retiring at the early age of fifty-six to Folkestone in Kent.

Incidentally, Sir Richard Branson's first enterprise, as a lad, was breeding and selling budgerigars and he has done quite well for himself.

So thank you to those budgerigars and their owners for the pleasure given, the lessons learnt and the big improvement in our way of life.

-4-

THE BEST ADVICE I EVER GOT

'It is more blessed to give than to receive'
(Acts 20:35)

My Dad never openly lectured or coached me, but occasionally suggested something that turned out to be really important and shaped my life. I'm glad I took those bits of advice and it makes me feel good to recall them now.

As a small boy, I would sit on Dad's lap in his special chair for my evening cuddle. He obviously loved us all and, when I grew up, I always gave Dad a kiss on the forehead whenever I saw him. I am glad I did so just before he died unexpectedly, when I was twenty-eight. The first tip I remember that he gave me was to work hard at school and try to pass my exams. This, he said quite simply, would lead to a good job, a good wage and I would not be harming my body with hard, physical work, like many men. He did not mention the sheer joy of learning great subjects like English, mathematics and biology, so that was a bonus from Dad's advice.

Dad later added, as I mentioned earlier, that I should try to avoid shift work, which he said interferes with your sleep pattern, meal times and family life. He blamed it for his indigestion and eventual gall stones. As I have said previously, he died in hospital following an operation to remove his gall bladder. Naturally, whether this advice was valid or not, I have never worked shifts. Fortunately, it has never been necessary.

He was always able to speak to people at all levels on a wide range of subjects and advised me to try to build as broad a knowledge as possible, so that I could make conversation with whoever I met. This I believe I have managed to achieve. I particularly remember being seated next to a very pleasant, elderly Lady Elizabeth Douglas-Home, wife of the former prime minister, at a meal in Eton College. I was representing my company, Lucas Industries, as a young manager trying to encourage sixth-formers to consider working in industry. Lady Douglas-Home was a charming person, born in 1909 the daughter of the headmaster of Eton College and the first woman to become a fellow or governor of Eton. Fortunately, we had a great time talking about garden plants and I was very comfortable in her company.

Dad was also quite willing to give presentations, mostly at his budgerigar society, and to speak up in public. He thought it was always worth trying things, otherwise you could miss important opportunities. I do not find public speaking a problem, as long as I am prepared and really know the subject. Most of my career has involved presenting cases for approval and I have rarely failed to persuade project boards and company directors to give me the required money. Dad would use this confidence on other occasions, such as when he was called for jury service. He had just become an insurance agent for the Cooperative Insurance Society and felt a great responsibility to his clients. When the potential jurors were asked whether there was any reason that they should not be selected, only Dad raised his hand. He explained that he was effectively self-employed and, as well as him losing income, his clients would not have valid insurance unless he collected their premium payments on time. He was immediately dismissed and all the others were chosen for service. Several jurors said to Dad afterwards that their situation was worse than his, but only he spoke up. He was not recommending dereliction of public duty, but simply speaking up for oneself.

Dad also advised me not to smoke. It was not until 1950 that Professors Doll and Hill (see later) published a paper showing the connection between smoking and various forms of ill health, but their findings were not universally accepted. However, when I was a small lad, Dad made it clear to me that although he smoked, as most men did, he strongly suggested that his children should not. He said it was addictive and a waste of money. He did not mention the supposedly unproven health issue, which the tobacco industry firmly denied. He said he would give up smoking, if the price went up in the budget again. It did, of course, so he stuck to his word and never smoked again, aged fifty-five, after forty years of cigarettes. I have never smoked and nor have my children. Thanks Dad.

Dad obviously had will power and one of my earliest memories was on this subject. As a small boy, I would get up several times a night to go to the toilet. One night I bumped into Dad. 'What are you up to?' he asked. 'You've already been to the loo two or three times.'

'I need to go again or I'll wet the bed,' I replied.

'No, you don't need to go,' he said.

'Yes, I do.' I retorted.

'Listen to me. Just tell yourself that you don't need to, because you've already been. It's called will power. Just do that and I promise that you won't wet the bed,' he said.

I remember he was very calm and kindly. Dad could get quite cross at times, but not on this occasion and I remember the difference. I just went back to bed and slept through. I do not think that I have got up in the night more than once or twice since then, but, more to the point, I learned about will power.

Although Dad had a motor bike as a young man, he warned me against having one. He said everybody fell off a bike and four wheels were safer than two. I never did bother with bikes. I deliberately gave my children driving lessons on their seventeenth birthdays to 'steer' them towards cars, not bikes. Neither rode a motor bike until my son bought one in 2008 to get him through the traffic to the train station, as he commuted to London. Within six months, a lady in a four-by-four managed to emerge from a side road and hit his bike and left leg. The machine was almost unmarked but his leg had a rather nasty break just below the knee. I know that motor bikes can be fun and useful to some folk, but I really do not think they are worth the risk.

Lastly, Dad told me to support Spurs (Tottenham Hotspur Football Club) as opposed to Arsenal. His reason was that Spurs were a skilful, sporting, attacking side, whereas Arsenal, the main alternative, were more defensive in style. If you do not enjoy football, read on anyway, as I have something to say. Many famous people in all walks of life, including popes, politicians and world acclaimed singers like Pavarotti and Julio Inglesias all played and enjoyed watching football. I recently heard the great journalist Kate Adie speaking on the twentieth anniversary of the dreadful incident in Tiananmen Square. On a much lighter note, she was asked her view on her football team, Sunderland FC, appointing a new manager, Steve Bruce. Her demeanour changed to that of an enthusiastic fan and I warmed to

Kate even more. Whether you are a rugby fan, an Arsenal fan or love only the arts, then please accept that none of us are right or wrong, but merely and thankfully different. Dad's dad had been an original Spurs fan, when they were formed, so it's in the blood, not a recent choice. What a joy when I started watching the great Spurs players, like Danny Blanchflower and Dave Mackay, and saw them do the league and cup "double" in 1961 (or have I already mentioned that?).

I recently saw a very old advertisement for cigarettes, showing a Spurs player smoking and advocating a certain brand as 'the sportsman's cigarette'. It's a funny old game.

-5-

THE COURTSHIP …
'KENNEDY SHOT DEAD? ARE YOU SURE?'

'Never frown…even when you're sad you never know when someone is falling in love with your smile'
(Anon)

'President Kennedy has just been shot dead,' said Ruth as she stepped from the bus, looking lovely in a bright orange blouse and short black skirt. She had her brown hair in the fashionable bob style. Very nice, I thought. We were meeting in Enfield town for our first proper date together and I must admit that I was quite surprised by her opening statement. We were going to the pictures to see West Side Story and it was, of course, 22nd November 1963.

'Kennedy shot dead? Are you sure?' I enquired, not realizing I was going out with one of the smartest people I'd ever meet, as well as being the one I would marry.

'Of course I'm sure,' she replied as we progressed to the cinema. You see, in those days, as far as I was aware, we didn't have assassinations. A little later, our activity in the back row was interrupted by a news flash on the screen that President John F. Kennedy had indeed been shot dead. Forty years later I was driven around Dallas by a good friend, who pointed out the route of the Kennedy entourage and the building from which he was allegedly shot that fateful day. My thoughts returned to my first date – a poignant day for me and the world.

So, how did I first meet the girl who would create such a happy life for me? Well, I attended Enfield Grammar School for boys and she attended Enfield County Grammar School for girls. Fortunately, the two buildings were only yards apart. When we were about fifteen years old and became interested in the opposite sex, a few of us lads would chat to a similar size group of girls. This developed into fairly innocent parties of a dozen or so youngsters, including me and Ruth. I do not know what she saw in me, but I saw dancing eyes, a lovely smile, great legs and a girl who always seemed so happy and alive.

Ruth told me she also supported Spurs, so several of us agreed to meet at their ground, White Hart Lane, to see a match. When I got there, the only other person to turn up was Ruth. I think it was a well-meaning conspiracy by our friends, who must have detected the chemistry. I bravely kissed her on the way home and it was a thrilling moment. The rest is not simply history, because I am going to tell you about it.

There was indeed some competition to go out with her, but I was determined and saw them off by staying as close to her as possible. Every day at school we would pass each other notes and meet for a walk in the park. I would spend every spare penny I had on nights out and bus fairs. I often wonder whether I was simply lucky to get her or whether I partly made my own luck by hanging onto her so doggedly. Either way, I got a fantastic result, for life. Forty-five years later, I produced a scrapbook of Ruth's life for her sixtieth birthday and our ruby wedding anniversary, which was on 28th September 2008. Here is a poem I wrote for the book:

What would I be without you?
Less than half the man.
What is it about you that
Loves me the way I am?
Your happiness, commitment, forgiveness,
Imagination, knowledge and GO!
Of all the people that I've met
You're still the best I know.

To everyone's surprise, except her, Ruth left school aged sixteen and did not enter the sixth form. She had done some voluntary work at a local hospital and decided to start her career. She wanted to enter her first job and study part-time to become a qualified medical laboratory technician. She had made up her mind and that was that, but it was also to earn some money and help us get started in married life a few years later.

I had a number of holiday jobs to raise some much needed cash. My parents were better off than when I was small, but now had to pay their mortgage, so I had little pocket money as such. I never bought much for myself, but there was the significant cost of visiting my girlfriend and taking her out. Fortunately I managed to find work in various local offices and industrial units. I calculated wages, operated machines and even helped an electrician to re-wire the ceiling of a factory, bending and threading the conduit pipes myself. In many ways the best job was with the Post Office delivering the Christmas mail. Many students were taken on for this period and the money was very good. I was certainly better paid than friends of mine who were labouring on building sites. I even got a tip from a Mrs Jolly. What a super name.

I wasn't really up to labouring as I had hurt my back playing tennis at school. I had quickly grown from one of the shortest in my class to be one of the tallest, but I was skinny and my back was not quite strong enough. The injury was described as a sprain and I was an outpatient at the North Middlesex Hospital for six months. Part of the therapy was to lie face down on the floor trying to throw a large heavy ball to other patients. I was sixteen and they were nearly all men in their forties, who had been injured at work. I did not consider my problem to be too serious and hoped for a complete cure, but there has always been some discomfort, great or small, lurking in my back. I never allowed that injury to stop me trying sports and doing my household duties, but would need occasional physiotherapy to straighten me up and alleviate the pain. I can feel it now, but I try to think of it as simply a bit of a nuisance.

Ruth and I often went to the pictures in Enfield and I would always see her home, right to her front door. This was a long, expensive trip for me with three bus rides and two lengthy walks, but worth every minute. I did stay at her house overnight occasionally, sleeping on a thin fold-up bed in their lounge. This was quite a performance, as it was difficult to get into the contraption without it tipping up and flinging the bedding across the room. I had to push footstools under each end to get some stability. There was no nearby table lamp, so I had to get into the bed in the dark, which made it even more of a challenge. In the winter, Ruth's mum would kindly pop into the room and put a large coat over me, as her rather nice house was just as cold as ours unfortunately. We all had ice on the inside, yes inside, of our windows before central heating become popular. Ruth's brother Dave, who was eleven years my senior and had a sense of fun, once informed me that he would be outside my door with a shotgun in case I attempted any hanky-panky with his sister! Together with his lovely wife Jean, we have been firm friends ever since.

Dad and my sister Colleen first met Ruth at a café with me in Enfield. They liked her straight away and it's rather touching that they told me so. I took that as a lesson and try to be open and sincere when I communicate with others. Colleen lived in Folkestone at this time and suggested that Ruth and I visit her and her husband Pat for a little holiday. We jumped at the chance, but needed parental permission. This was to be achieved by our parents all meeting for the first time and having a discussion about us. My Dad thought Ruth's parents Syd and Ethel were the kind of folk it would be nice to have as friends, so that pleased me. The key thing was that Ruth's parents agreed to the holiday!

We had a great time in Folkestone with Colleen and Pat, really discovering how it was to relax together. We romped around the sandy beach, went in the sea, took photographs and held hands a lot. I was so lucky to have a girlfriend. Colleen later told us the content of a sealed envelope that Ruth had handed to her from Ethel. The letter said, 'Dear Colleen, Please keep an eye on them, as they are so very young'. Ethel and Syd Browning were kind and loving people. My sister had to go to work each day, but she felt sure that we were being good. Good? We were excellent.

-6-

UNIVERSITY LIFE … 'THE FIRST 500'

'A professor is one who talks in someone else's sleep.'
(W.H. Auden, 1950)

In October 1965, my fellow students and I waited outside Eliot College at the brand new University of Kent at Canterbury. Most of us had no trendy new clothing and dressed very much like sixth formers. I thought we were a dull-looking bunch and, in my grey trousers and brown jacket, I was possibly the worst dressed of the lot. We were waiting because the college building was so recently completed that the floors had not dried from a final cleaning and we simply could not go in. When I had my interview a year earlier, the university consisted of an old farmhouse on a building site, where a hilltop farm once stood. By 1965 it had another two buildings, namely Eliot College and the part-finished physics building. The library was split between a portakabin at Beverley Farm and Eliot's Junior Common Room, until the first phase of a permanent building could open a year later. As with Oxford and Cambridge, Kent was built on a self-contained collegiate system. We were eventually able to enter Eliot, the first of several planned colleges, and those of us in residence hurried to locate our study bedrooms. There was quite a buzz in the air. My floor was not completely dry, but I was excited and I leapt from the doorway onto the bed. We were 'the first 500'.

I immediately made some pals, like my neighbour Peter, who would later turn out to be life-long friends. I still see some of them every year or two. It transpired that Pete and I both had dads who were agents for the Co-operative Insurance Society or CIS, so there was a coincidence and an immediate bond. An early problem that I had to sort out was that I saw my name on a list to study maths with physics. Oh no. I had specifically ticked a box to study maths with economics, which was the only other choice for mathematicians. I was greeted with, 'We assumed that as you did maths and physics at A level, you had ticked the wrong box.' I replied, 'No, would you please switch me to economics, as I want to try something different.' I actually felt trapped with maths and physics, which seemed just like more applied maths. I had always been channelled into the 'sciences' and really needed something to widen my horizons, so I got my way. No disrespect to physics, but I was getting enough theory and formulae with maths.

Some inventive young students (and almost all of us were just eighteen years old – not 'mature' students like nowadays) had decided to start some clubs. They had set up colourful stalls in the central hall or dining room. I joined the folk club, chess club and archery. The folk club was the only gathering for those interested in music, but the style did not suit me, so I dropped out. I had been good at chess at school, so I was pleased to play something at which I might succeed. My most memorable success and biggest disappointment was against the well-established Canterbury Chess Club. I was the university team's third best player, so I was on board three out of our team of six. Our opponents were most apologetic that for the first time in their history they could only bring five players, so we were immediately one point up. My friend Alan was a naturally bright chap and, unlike most of us, did not have to study very hard. He played on board six, so, having no opponent, he had to simply watch the games. Within five minutes, goodness knows how, I had beaten my opponent. At about forty years of age, he was their youngest player and clearly mortified at his defeat. However, he smiled, shook my hand and requested another game, which would not count in the overall contest. Scared stiff that he would justifiably thrash me, I accepted anyway, and beat him again before anyone else had finished their scheduled matches! So, you see, I was thrilled, especially as we won another game and drew one. Thanks to the 'bye' on board six, we won the contest by three and a half points to two and a half. Imagine how annoyed I felt a few days later when I read the report in the local paper, which ended with, 'Larry Brooks got a bye on board six, when his opponent failed to turn up'.

The archery was something brand new to me. A quiet, unassuming student named Barry organised the practice and we fired simple bows at traditional round targets. He taught us well and I could hit the target every time, if not the actual bull's-eye. Barry was keen on safety and had to explain more than once to another lad named Asif that he must point the arrow down until he was ready to fire. There was an astonishing occasion when Barry was setting up the targets some distance away and the rest of us were getting prepared for the session. Asif was chatting in an animated fashion and innocently, but dangerously, waving his loaded bow about. I could hardly believe it when he accidentally released the bow string and the arrow sailed through the air towards Barry. In the distance we were horrified to see the arrow hit Barry in the chest. He did not fall, but removed it and walked slowly towards us. 'Now, Asif,' he said calmly, 'that's why I told you not to point the arrow upwards until you are ready to fire.' It was surely the understatement of the year, but what a good guy and what a lesson in calm, constructive criticism. I felt so glad that the arrow had lost speed and only penetrated Barry's outer coat.

One notable club that I decided not to join was the Tiddlywinks Society. They were an unusual bunch who carried rolled up rubber mats under their arms for spontaneous games in unexpected places. I particularly liked one of their posters, which proclaimed, 'All winkers, tiddly or otherwise, are invited to play for the Prince Philip Silver Wink'.

After some months at university, my previously short black hair with a side parting grew into the same shaggy style that the Beatles were sporting at the time and I was quite pleased with it. I looked like a student, it kept me warm and cost little to maintain. As I was a fan of the Beatles, that worked out quite well.

I had not been one for reading fiction and thought there was too little time, but I soon realised that I was less well-read than my friends. Many of us then read the popular 'Brave New World' by Aldous Huxley and '1984' by George Orwell, which made me a big fan of Orwell's books. On the coursework booklist of some of my pals was Howards End by E.M.Forster, so I read that too. Nowadays, Ruth and I collect Victorian prints from paintings by a nineteenth century artist named Maud Goodman, so when I picked up Howards End again in 1999, I was amazed to find that Forster mentions 'One of the masterpieces of Maud Goodman', which was hanging in the house that he was describing. The author also inscribed 'only connect' on the title page, as he valued personal relationships so highly, as do I.

Despite all the study and fun, like drinking parties, my main 'hobby' was seeing Ruth at every opportunity. She became well-known and accepted among my friends on her frequent visits. It is no disrespect to the girls at university, but there is nobody like Ruth.

At the end of my first year in Eliot College, I had the choice of living in digs or moving into the second, newly constructed college called Rutherford. Like Eliot, it was built so that you could stand at the entrance and look right through the building to the huge dining room window and see the splendid Canterbury Cathedral perfectly framed. I chose Rutherford, knowing that it meant my third year would definitely be spent in accommodation in the wider community. My good friend Pete followed suit and in our third year we went into digs in the nearby village of Blean with the marvellous Mrs Kidd. Pete had a very old and very soft bed in his room and I can clearly remember popping my head round his door to say goodnight. His mattress was so soft that he could lie in it with his 'head showing, but no other visible sign that it was occupied', in his own words.

Mrs Kidd was a widow in her seventies and a real live wire. The first impact she made was to cook us the most splendid breakfasts, which were different every day for two weeks. I had never even heard of kedgeree before she presented us with it. Delicious. Once she got to know us she told us how her husband had passed away. They were both pillars of the church, involved with Kent County Cricket Club and very active in the community. One day they were gardening and she walked from the back garden to the front to offer her husband a cup of tea. He was lying on the path, having died from a heart attack. She was so upset that they had not been able to say goodbye and it shook her faith in God that such an unkind thing should happen.

It was obvious how much she loved her husband, who had been born in Avoca, County Wicklow in Ireland. Avoca is also the small town where the popular BBC television series Ballykissangel was filmed. In Mrs Kidd's front garden, close to the road, she had a swinging, creaking sign with the name 'Avoca' painted on it in white on a black background. I arrived at the house from university late one evening and my dear landlady was most upset that the sign had gone. That quite annoyed me and I set off to look for it. I wondered whether it had been snatched by somebody returning from a nearby pub and thrown away, so I started my search in the opposite direction from the pub. I looked both sides of the road and soon spotted it in a hedge less than twenty yards away. It slightly disturbed me that I could deduce what a vandal would do, but Mrs Kidd was very relieved and pleased to get it back.

Mrs K was very excited one afternoon and was bursting to impart to us a little bit of humour. She had a nesting box for birds in her pretty back garden and a family of blue tits was developing nicely inside. Unfortunately, a cat had climbed up and was trying to put its paw in the hole. According to Mrs K, she ran to the neighbours for help, shouting, 'The cat's got my tits!' She roared with laughter and slapped her thighs in delight at this risqué little tale. She was such a nice lady that we later invited her to our wedding and she accepted with pleasure, despite it being seventy miles away. My sister kindly collected her from Blean that day.

Despite being more academic than sporting, Pete and I became very good at table football or 'rods', beating almost all comers. We only played doubles with Pete in attack and me in defence, holding two rods each. One day, Pete stunned me with the suggestion that, because we were so good, we should give others a chance by swapping defence and attack. I had practically never played in attack and at first said 'No.' As it was going to be attack or nothing, I eventually agreed, but felt absolutely hopeless in that position. It is remarkable that after a few defeats, we were once again champions. I am so glad Pete did that, as it taught me to be a bit more daring. Then a really amazing thing happened. The table football machines were replaced with new ones, but you now had to flick the rods forward with your leading hand instead of backwards. Several of us felt we had no power or control in that mode and just could not master it, so we actually stopped playing altogether. It showed me that a fairly innocent and unnecessary change can really upset things. I remembered this later in life when my career moved into 'change management'. I always made sure that I consulted the 'users' first and clearly explained the change in detail.

The social life at university was excellent. Parties revolved around drinking too much 'rough cider' at four old pence a pint. As I had a ground floor study bedroom for my first two years, my window was used as an unofficial entrance and exit to the building. This was for either resident students, who had stayed out too late, or non-residents, who got locked in when the main door was shut at night. Two fellow students married shortly after university and I met up with them again at the twenty-five year reunion. They had decided to book his old bedroom for the night to see whether they could still both fit into a two foot six inches wide bed! (The technique is for the chap to sleep on the edge with one hand on the floor to stop him falling out, or so I am told).

I was not good enough at football to make the university team, but two of my best mates, Bob and Dave, were regulars. I followed the team and they had some very good players, once reaching the semi-finals of the Universities Athletics Union (UAU) cup. This is where you play the likes of Loughborough, who were recognised internationally for their sporting excellence, whereas this was our first year of entry. We narrowly lost the semi-final and went out of the cup, but the lads had done very well. We thought we had a good team, so we arranged a friendly game against Fulham FC's reserves. They were mostly youngsters, except for an aging Terry Dyson, who I had seen play many times for Spurs and score some great goals. The first thing I noticed from the touchline was that their thighs were bigger than our chests. The game was played at breakneck speed, by Fulham, and I think we got into their half only a few times. We almost had an attack following a very long ball from defence, but it came to nothing. Fulham won by seven goals to nil. The difference in class between amateur and professional sport was huge.

Initially, Pete was not a great football fan, but decided that as it interested his new pals so much, he would become more involved. We supported his endeavours and went with him to see his local team, Charlton Athletic at The Valley. Unfortunately, they lost, but Pete and his family, including his dad and brother, became life-long, dedicated fans. Pete later said that I introduced him to the 'unwavering tribal loyalty of the real football supporter'.

One of my other friends, Colin, was a very strong fellow, who regularly worked out in the gym. He would amaze me by performing one-handed press-ups! He was also smart and studied hard to achieve a first class honours degree in physics. Believe me, that's not easy. When I met up with him and his family some years later, his wife described how he was under his car, doing some maintenance, when the jack slipped and the car fell on his chest. He managed to keep breathing while neighbours lifted the vehicle and eased him free. Thanks to his sheer strength, he suffered no long-term damage.

Under the university campus is a disused railway tunnel and I went down there once to see the rifle-shooting team in action. Some years later, I was tutoring maths part-time for the Open University to earn some extra money. One evening I drove down to the university to see some students in the Gulbenkian Theatre and it had collapsed! Some red and white warning tapes were strung across the closed entrance and an explanatory note was hanging from it. The old tunnel had given way and the ground subsided. Not only was I unable to tutor my students, but the university computer, containing examination results, was trapped inside the closed and dangerous building for quite some time. Incidentally, the main reason for the collapse was put down to the drying out and shrinking of the soil. Having once been farmland, it was now concreted over and rain water simply did not penetrate the ground, but ran off the perimeter of the large site, before draining away.

Whilst at university, I spent two summer vacations working in a public library in north London and lived with Ruth's parents, as mine were living in Folkestone. I learned an interesting lesson whilst meeting and serving the public. I stamped a lady's books one day and, as usual, said, 'Thank you, madam.' Lunchtime found me in the baker's shop across the road. 'Thank you, sir,' said that same lady, as I bought some buns. We are all at times somebody's customer or servant.

The head librarian, like many people, was an ex-serviceman (a sergeant-major to be exact). He could be a bit authoritarian and I did not think he was a sports fan, so I was a little nervous in 1966 when I asked for half a day off to watch the football World Cup Final between England and West Germany on television. He surprised me by agreeing, so I bussed and ran to my house that Saturday in July to see the game with Ruth and my Dad. Unfortunately my favourite player, Jimmy Greaves, was not selected for the match. However, we all know the outcome and it is yet another rare thing I have been fortunate enough to witness in my lifetime. I am still waiting for a repeat of England winning the final. Maybe next time.

We had a television room in Eliot College, which was packed every Thursday at seven o'clock for University Challenge followed by Top of the Pops. There were a few chairs, but most of us sprawled untidily around the floor, as students do. There was great excitement in 1967 when a colour television arrived and the BBC started a scheduled broadcasting service in this amazing innovation. The sexy, all-girl dance group Pan's People were even more interesting in the pink. The colours were unstable at first and we all had to be careful not to disturb the TV otherwise an 'expert' would have to leap up and make it viewable again. Red was very bright, particularly if the programme was imported from the USA. It was hardly HD!

During my three years in Canterbury, there were two very notable events, which affected some of us deeply. We were fortunate young men and women with few cares and our whole lives ahead of us. Then we got news of the Aberfan disaster. On Friday 21 October 1966, after several days of heavy rain, a subsidence occurred on the colliery waste tip above the village of Aberfan in Wales. An enormous, sickening landslide destroyed a farm and twenty terraced houses. It then hit the side of the junior school and part of the separate senior school, filling the classrooms with thick mud and rubble up to ten metres deep. It claimed 144 lives, including 116 children. One of my Welsh friends, a tall rugby playing chap, just broke down and cried when he heard the awful news. Somehow this struck me almost as much as the terrible incident itself, probably because I could see him, but I could not imagine all those poor little children dying like that. Many years later, Ruth and I happened to be driving quite near to Aberfan. After some discussion on whether or not we were intruding, we decided to visit the cemetery. Well, it was as sad and moving as I expected.

On 5th June 1967 there commenced another staggering event, the Six-Day War. It was also known as the Arab-Israeli War. I must say that I was surprised when Jewish students, both boys and girls, declared that they were actually flying out to fight for Israel. This sort of conflict was a complete mystery to lucky, naïve little me. Suddenly the war was over, before my friends had left Britain. Israel had defeated the armies of Egypt, Syria and Jordan in six days. I do hate war. It may be necessary at times, but I hate it.

On a much lighter note, but with its scary moment, was my first of many trips to Bonnie Scotland. My best friend, Pete, had organised a youth hostelling holiday for us plus his girlfriend Margaret and Ruth. This was fascinating to me as I had never imagined being able to arrange a trip of some complexity like that, but Pete is a very clever chap. The holiday went very well, even though youth hostel accommodation was single-sex. We also had to do chores at each site, like cleaning the rather grubby toilets. We saw Glasgow, the beautiful Loch Lomond and the splendid Isle of Arran. The ferryman who took us across Loch Lomond to Rowardennan was a distinctive, slim young man, who we were to see several more times in his various guises. After we landed, he collected a uniform and sack and cycled past us as the island postman. Later, he was the barman in the local hostelry. Finally, of course, he ferried us back. It seems that if you live on an island, you may find it necessary to do several jobs to earn a living. The four of us looked very young, but as we approached the ferry from Dunoon to Arran, we were still surprised to be bundled aboard with a group of schoolchildren, without being asked to pay. Whilst on Arran, we decided to climb Goat Fell, the highest point on the island. Normally, it would not be a great feat, but as we climbed, a fierce and freezing mist swept down the mountain. We stuck together and carried on until we were so cold and it was such a thick mist that we could not see, hear or think. We were beginning to get a bit scared and it seemed unnecessarily dangerous to go on. It was with reluctance, but relief that we turned back, soaked and very cold. Luckily, we found the path down and no permanent harm was done.

I must say a little more about what I was studying at university. Having passed my part one exams, I progressed to the second and final part. Again I had to choose a subject to go with the pure maths, so I opted for statistics. My hope was that it would be more practical and intelligible than mathematical theory, which was just about driving me to distraction. I am pleased to say that I enjoyed statistics and wrote a most interesting thesis for my finals. It concerned the statistical relationship between smoking and various forms of ill health, like cancer and heart disease. In 1950, two professors Doll and Hill produced a statistical paper indicating that smoking actually caused a number of illnesses and huge numbers of deaths. In 1967, when I contacted these gentlemen for information, the tobacco lobby was still denying this, claiming that the kinds of people that smoked were also prone to cancer and other illnesses, so smoking was not the cause. We all know this to be nonsense now, but I knew it then. The facts were horrific. The more you smoked, the greater your chances of many dreadful forms of ill health and death. However, if you gave it up, the risk of most problems would reduce to that of a non-smoker within about ten years.

Considering that this was university in the 1960s with hippies and flower-power, you may be wondering about drug-taking. Well, call me naïve or protected, but I never thought about nor saw any drugs, let alone take them and that is something that pleases me.

Before I finished university in 1968, my entire family had transferred to Folkestone, but I never did. The move from Edmonton to Folkestone happened quite quickly. It started with my elder sister Colleen meeting a chap at a bus stop in London. Mum was with Colleen at the time and nudged her, telling her to say hello, because he was such a handsome fellow. She did and he introduced himself as Pat Smith from Folkestone, currently working in London. They made a very attractive couple and Pat turned out to be a real gentleman, not so much by birth, but by nature. They married and moved to Folkestone, where we would have little holidays.

Colleen would sometimes drive to the university in Canterbury and take me out for a treat. She bought me my first Chinese meal and I can still clearly see us finishing the lot. Students, like Brookses, were always hungry. I have been hooked on Chinese food ever since. Fortunately, we have an excellent restaurant and an even better takeaway near our present home.

My brother and wife also moved to Folkestone, shortly followed by Mum, Dad and Marilyn, then aged fifteen. Whilst my parents were looking for a bungalow to buy, Dad showed me details of two properties that he was considering. One was modern with three bedrooms and a little garden, whereas the other was older with character, two bedrooms and a big garden that merged into trees and hillside. He asked my opinion. I could tell that he wanted the latter, but his dilemma was around me and the fact that it had only two bedrooms. I immediately suggested that he bought the older property as I would not be living there anyway. I would live with Ruth's parents during university holidays and marry as soon as I graduated. He did buy the older bungalow, but I realise now that I was effectively announcing that I was moving out, permanently. I know they missed me, but I only realised how much when my own son did almost exactly the same thing and I certainly missed him.

The day my parents moved to Folkestone, Marilyn was due to take part in her school sports day. Colleen had come up to Edmonton by train to look after Marilyn on her last day and take her to the new family home. Marilyn was taking part in several field and track events, ending with the relay race. Colleen was getting frantic as they were in danger of missing the last train, but Marilyn was due to run the final leg of the relay. In order to speed up her departure with Colleen, Marilyn was switched to run the first leg. As she handed over the baton, Colleen grabbed her hand and they raced for the train. To this day, Marilyn does not know who won the relay!

One sunny day Marilyn and I went for a walk up the rather steep Sugar Loaf hill in Folkestone. On the way down, Marilyn was running too fast and yelling for help. There was real danger of a disastrous tumble and I shouted to her to sit down, which she somehow did immediately. She later wrote in a scrapbook that Ruth compiled for me that I had saved her life. Her life is very precious and as I write this chapter in April 2009, she has completed chemotherapy for breast cancer and has started radiotherapy. Marilyn has never smoked, keeps fit, eats the correct food and there is no known family history of cancer. When I said she was the last person I would expect to get cancer, she simply said, 'Somebody's got to get it. It happens to be me. Even children get it and they certainly don't deserve it'. She is great and so positive about overcoming this curse. To keep you up-to-date, she was signed off by the oncologist in May 2009, with star pupil status, and says she feels as though she never had cancer in the first place!

There were many good times in Folkestone, but I recall an occasion when Dad and I were walking his dogs along the sea front. He had two poodles and five whippets. He had always loved whippets, having had one called Nippy when he was a boy in east London. However, it was the surprisingly tough poodle bitch called Freda that fell into the rough sea. We were walking on a stone promenade high above the water with no steps down for a great distance. She was swimming bravely and being pushed against the sea wall, but could not make it to the safety of some distant steps. Dad's solution was fantastic. He took most of the dogs' leads and tied them together. The handle of the last one was twisted into a loop and this was lowered towards Freda. Dad spent a considerable time on his knees trying to get the loop over Freda's head, until he eventually succeeded. It was just as well that Freda was strong and Dad was determined, as he pulled her to the steps and safety. She simply shook the seawater from her coat, the way dogs do, and off we went.

Anyway, back to university and despite distractions, like a permanent, non-student girlfriend that I wanted to see at the weekends, I managed to gain a Bsc (Hons) Maths & Economics. Hooray, I could get a job, buy a house and marry Ruth! As my son says, it was 'job done'.

In order to celebrate our success, about a dozen of my student friends and I went to the amusement park in Margate known then as Dreamland. All went well until my mate Dave and I got on the double Ferris wheel that was one huge wheel on top of another one of equal size, like a giant bicycle rearing upwards to the sky. We were ushered onto this rather old wooden seat at ground level by a very young lad, who did not fill me with confidence. He casually swung a metal bar across our laps and secured it, if that's the word, with a pin going through two holes. The metal bar was very weak and wobbly and the seat rocked backwards and forwards quite wildly as we jerked upwards to allow people onto the next set of seats. We were now rising on the revolving lower wheel and felt very unsafe and quite frightened as we were nearly tipped out of the back. I think we originated the white knuckle ride as we gripped the bar and framework of this horrible thing. The turning wheel was bad enough, but then it quickly changed positions with the upper wheel, which is spine-chilling to recall. We were now rocking in this open-backed seat and spinning on the top wheel many, many feet above the ground. In a brief moment of clarity I saw France across the English Channel. Then the worst moment occurred, our seat stopped at the very top with a sudden jolt and swung violently.

Dave, who was as scared as I was, said, 'Larry, that's the first time I have heard you swear in the three years I have known you.' Due to a technical fault or staff incompetence we remained rocking to and fro at the very top for a further twenty minutes, by which time I was so paralysed with fear, that I cannot remember the journey back down to land. Our friends, who were tiny dots among the throngs from our vantage point were hard to find after the incident, as they assumed we had left. It did rather spoil the evening, but Dave remains a friend.

As well as Ruth's love and support throughout my university days, I so clearly remember Mum and Dad's pride at the degree ceremony in Eliot College. The elegant Princess Marina handed me my certificate with the magnificent Canterbury Cathedral highlighted through the huge window behind her. Dad's smile was like the cat that got the cream, which indeed he had afterwards, with strawberries.

Canterbury and Folkestone have been and remain important places for me with some very happy memories.

-7-

NO, YOU CAN'T GET ENGAGED

'How do I love thee? Let me count the ways.'
(Elizabeth Barrett Browning, 1840)

Whilst still in the school sixth form in 1965, it had become quite clear that Ruth was the only girl for me. She was and still is the underlying source of all my happiness. We had decided that before I left for university that September, we would get engaged. I was eighteen and Ruth almost seventeen, when we approached her parents.

'We'd like to get engaged now and married in three years time, when I leave university,' I explained.

'No, it's too early,' Ruth's parents simply replied. 'Wait and see how you feel after a year away at university.'

We were shocked and disappointed, but did as we were told. In those days you asked for permission to marry and, generally, got the desired result. As going away to university had only strengthened my love for Ruth, we were allowed to get engaged the following year on 28th September 1966, Ruth's eighteenth birthday.

The plan was to get my degree in July 1968, start work the same month, find a house, secure a mortgage and marry on 28th September. Good plan, so I had to line up a job. It may seem odd in these days of numerous different career options, but many of my university pals saw the only possible jobs were either to teach what they had just learned or become graduate social workers. I did not see myself doing either and looked into accountancy, operational research and actuarial work. Sadly, they all seemed to involve a lot more study and did not actually interest me. There was no such thing as a degree in computing and the few companies with computer departments did not visit the universities to interview for graduate positions. It was by chance that I stumbled into computing and Business Systems Analysis as a profession.

My future father-in-law, Sydney Browning, had been a director of a fruit importing firm in London's Covent Garden. Following a serious illness, he was pleased to accept a job managing a toy shop in Palmers Green, north London. He enjoyed this and was very good at it, despite the inconvenience of an operation for colitis and other health issues. I know Syd liked me and he was kind enough to offer me some holiday work in the shop. It was there that a customer of Syd's suggested that I apply for the position of systems analyst in the computer department of a firm named J&E Hall Ltd in Dartford, Kent. I applied, was interviewed and got it, with the proviso that I obtained a degree, so that was the job lined up for July 1968.

We had also started the process of buying a house in Kent, which we would have to get ready for us to move in when we got married in September. As I mentioned earlier, Fred Corney gave us some help and early in July we found a modern semi-detached house on an attractive estate near Gravesend. It had a garage, a brick and glass entrance porch, three bedrooms and a 'through lounge' with plenty of natural light. We really wanted it, but alas at £4750 it was about £300 too expensive for us. We would be permitted a mortgage of three times my salary and the rest would have to be a cash deposit. As all my savings and holiday pay had gone to fund university, I had nothing to contribute and there were no loans available without collateral security. Ruth had worked and saved every penny she could, but unfortunately it was not enough. Strangely, houses priced around £4450, which we could afford, were far inferior and generally in less desirable locations, like next to a railway line. We were actually very lucky to be looking at houses at all, as most young couples rented a flat. Also, obtaining the mortgage depended on getting the job, which itself had depended on obtaining my degree, but hey ho. I hope you are keeping up.

In the meantime, Ruth had applied for a laboratory technician job at the Brook Hospital in Woolwich, south London, to commence in October 1968. She was successful, of course. I could not see her failing an interview with her brains and personality.

We had a daring plan to get the house we wanted. We asked both our dads whether they could each lend us £150, which we promised to repay within six months. They very kindly agreed and that meant we could buy our semi in Gravesend! We did pay them back as planned, but that involved saving every penny and buying nothing but essentials. We did not bother with a television at first, for example. We were too busy decorating anyway. Colours like dove grey and cream were popular for walls, so we went for those. I also painted the wooden part of the porch roof in navy blue and white vertical stripes (Spurs colours) but Ruth thought it looked like a beach hut and she was quite right, so I made it all blue. She likes beach huts nowadays.

We would not, of course, live together before marriage. There was no question of that in those days. Apart from any moral issues, you were bombarded with scary warnings about venereal disease or VD and nobody wanted that. However, we visited the house as often as possible to get things straight before the wedding and that was very exciting for us. Then there occurred the most devastating rain and flooding across north-west Kent. Whilst our new house was on high ground, all the roads around Gravesend and Dartford, where I worked, were badly flooded. We rang Ruth's parents and pointed out, rather than asked permission, that we would have to spend the night in the new house. As we were soon to marry, it was acceptable.

That flooding caused dreadful damage in Dartford with many residents losing their belongings and shops having all their stock ruined. I remember seeing goldfish from the town park swimming along the high street. I was in a small boat at the time, being ferried from the railway station to the office.

We were married at St Thomas church in Oakwood, north London, close to Ruth's home. As planned, the date was 28th September 1968, Ruth's twentieth birthday. It was a very traditional wedding with many friends, relatives and neighbours. My friend Peter was best man and the bridesmaids, dressed in sky blue, were my sister Marilyn and Ruth's best friend Sheila. Two university pals, Bob and Dave, were ushers and our nephew Mark was a dear little three year old page boy in black trousers, smart white shirt and blue cummerbund to match the bridesmaids' dresses. Ruth's mother made us a tiered wedding cake with two little people standing on the top, a bride and groom looking just like us. Ruth's aunt Sally made the bridesmaids' dresses and the beautiful, elegant white wedding dress with a pretty little hat and delicate veil. Ruth looked radiant and smiled throughout. Sally worked as a haute couture dressmaker for the Hardy Amies fashion company, so she really knew her stuff. She was also my wife's godmother, so things could not have been better, especially as Ruth's dear dad Syd gave her away. It was a happy day, but I can remember very little due to my nervousness, which I largely hid. It is still the best day of my life, especially when we drove our little old car away to start our honeymoon.

Our first night was spent in the Wessex Hotel, in the grounds of the stunning Winchester Cathedral. Fortunately it was pre-paid and Ruth's brother Dave had ordered a bottle of champagne for our room. Incidentally, as this book is about happiness, I will tell you that sex makes me extremely happy, but I will be giving no details, of course. Anyway, it was a wonderful evening and we emerged from the room sometime the next day to make our way to Cornwall for a few days. Unfortunately, at check-out, I could not shake off a smartly dressed porter, who grabbed our case. I could foresee, with dread, the need for a tip. The problem was that we were on a very tight budget that did not allow for tips. Even worse was the fact that the only coin I had was a half crown (or twelve and a half pence nowadays). This was too much for a tip, but we had nothing else and I could not get my case from him politely.

The most embarrassing moments followed, as we trudged through the car park. 'Is this your car?' he would enquire, as we passed every gleaming limousine. I shook my head, resigned to him actually wanting to take our case right up to the car. Eventually, we stopped beside our dear little 1952 Morris Minor, showing his age and quite some rust. I did not look up as the porter put our case in the boot and I parted with the half crown, which I had been gripping so tightly that it made a red mark in my hand. I just had to accept what had happened and drive off, hoping for no more such incidents. By the way, the car was known to us as Poop, after the noise made by its horn. Ruth's dad had given his little girl the car when she passed her driving test, first time, of course, aged seventeen.

We had a good time driving around Cornwall, visiting Land's End and the rugged Cornish coast for the first time. Now, I pride myself in being a good planner, but as we began the journey home, we seemed to have spent a pound or so more than we had budgeted. There were no credit cards in those days and I cannot think why we had no cheque book with us. They certainly existed, because we had a new joint bank account with the National Provincial. Perhaps there was no money in it or we had not been sent the book.

We had scheduled the last night of our honeymoon to be somewhere in Somerset and found a rather spooky old pub with very basic accommodation, but it was cheap enough for us to take a room. It was getting dark and the landlord had a black patch over one eye, which added to the atmosphere. Fortunately, his wife seemed very nice and cooked us one of the best steak meals I have ever eaten. It was not expensive, but we began to worry as we started our long journey home the next morning with only six shillings to our name. Fortunately we had eaten a hearty breakfast. Petrol was five shillings (twenty-five pence) a gallon and we needed an additional three gallons to get home, so we did not have enough money. However, by lunchtime we were incredibly thirsty and had to squander a shilling on a glass of lemonade, which we shared. Things were looking grim and I do not think we really knew what to do. It seems pathetic now.

Then a miracle happened. We stopped at a garage to buy one gallon of petrol with our five shillings. I was about to trudge back to the car wondering how far we would get, when the lady handed me a scratch card, which was free with every gallon. You had to rub off five squares out of ten and form a word from the letters. Success would win you ten shillings or, in my terms, the two gallons of petrol we needed to get home.

Ruth touched my arm and looked over my shoulder as I rubbed off the squares. This was our only hope and I had to be positive. An X was followed by a P. My heart sank. Then it was L, I and finally O. Suddenly, with inspiration and great excitement, I said to Ruth, 'Is there an oxlip? There's a cowslip, but is there an oxlip?' We were unsure, but I bravely wrote oxlip on the card and gave it to the lady. 'There you are,' she said, handing over ten shillings. 'Two gallons of petrol please,' I replied, handing it back. Oxlip is still one of my favourite words. I hope you like it too. I have them growing in the wild part of my garden.

The next year, we were in the West Country visiting Ruth's brother Dave and family, when there was a loud noise above our heads. We stopped the Morris Minor and got out of the car. When we looked up, we saw a spectacular, long, white aeroplane with its nose in the dipped position flying really rather low. It was 9th April 1969 and test pilot Brian Trubshaw was making his first flight in the British-built prototype Corcorde. We felt surprised and privileged to see that historic event.

A little later in 1969, we sold our dear old car and bought a much newer Hillman Imp, which we took to Wales for a short break. Just outside Pontypool, I realised that my accelerator pedal was doing nothing and the car came to a halt by the side of the road. Puzzled, I looked underneath to see whether the accelerator cable might be broken, as I had heard of this happening with other cars. I did know, as you might also be aware, that the Imp's engine is in the boot, so I also looked in there. I did indeed find a broken cable flapping about and it was extremely long, as it had to reach from the front of the car to the back. The road was a bit isolated and we did not have access to a telephone, but a motorist stopped and suggested that we acquired a piece of wire and joined the broken ends of the cable back together. He seemed sensible enough, so I searched around some old farm fencing and pulled up a dirty, but detached length of wire. I think that Ruth and I were both somewhat surprised when I managed to mend the break by twisting the new piece into the cable and we drove off. I did, of course, get a new cable fitted in the next town. We later joined the Automobile Association.

While Ruth was working at the Brook Hospital, she needed her car, so I travelled to my job in Dartford by bus and train. Coming home, I would finally alight from the bus and walk to my house. The only way I could recognise it in a long road full of modern semis was by its cracked 'picture window'. My neighbour John, a roofing contractor, was very sociable and always whistling happily, so I asked his advice about the broken window. I had no experience of home ownership or maintenance and he seemed like a man of the world.

'Don't worry,' he said confidently, 'I'll get my man, old John, to sort it out for you.'

'Thanks', I said. 'What will it cost?'

'About four quid for the glass,' he replied.

'What about paying old John?' I enquired.

'He'll do it for a drink,' he replied.

I relayed this conversation to Ruth and she was happy enough with it. The next day I was walking home, but I could not see the cracked window. Instead, as I reached my house, I saw a man that I did not recognise standing in my lounge painting the window frame.

'You must be John,' I said cheerily, letting myself in through the locked front door; 'How did you manage to get in?'

He smiled and explained that he had removed the glass from the outside and climbed in.

'I'll have to buy you a drink,' I said and there began the most incredible drinking experience of my life.

'Young John' and I agreed to meet in our shared driveway at seven o'clock the next evening for the drink. I got home from work and changed from my suit into casual clothes. John got home from work and changed from his roofing clothes into a suit and we met in the driveway. We looked at one another and could see the humour in it. John, some fifteen years my senior, made nearly all the decisions. It started gently as he drove us a hundred yards to the pub on the estate. Walking to that venue was my only suggestion all evening, but John chose to drive for some reason. I had just enough money to buy three pints of bitter, which was what most men drank before lager became popular. Despite it being up to me to buy a drink as thanks for the new window, John beat me to the bar and insisted on buying the first pint. Apparently, we were to meet old John in Gravesend town centre, a few miles away, and I would be able to buy him a drink then. I noticed that young John bought three pints, but swiftly downed one at the bar, before we sat down. Within five minutes, he was back at the bar ordering two more pints. I finished my first pint very quickly and tried to keep up with John during my second one, but he was well ahead. Luckily he went to the toilet while I manfully downed my second.

Before I knew it, we were in a pub in Gravesend with old John and I managed to buy that pint I had promised. I also rang Ruth from the bar. There were no mobiles in those days, although I was later to become one of the first mobile phone users in Britain. Anyway, I told Ruth that I was having a lovely time and would probably be home later than I had originally thought, but had no money, so I could not squander what little we had to live on. Before this evening, the most that I had ever drunk in one session was four pints of cider at a pub near the university in Canterbury. In Gravesend, I remember two more pints in that pub, bought by the Johns of course, before we drove to a pub in Woolwich, some distance away in south London. Being a mathematician, I was counting how many pints I had drunk. I was not able to do much else. After my eleventh pint, I remember young John rescuing me from an altercation with a man and driving us at speed to yet another pub. Yes, John was still driving after, I imagine, fifteen pints. The pub had a cowboy theme and music. I had not experienced that sort of thing before and was not impressed, but I was blind drunk and could not really care. I managed to persuade the Johns to just buy me halves, but after nine halves I lost count, so my grand total was at least fifteen and a half pints. That may have been the finish, but I really don't know. John must have exceeded twenty pints when he drove us home, some fifteen miles. I had one of those brief moments of photographic clarity, when John drove onto the middle of a grassy roundabout on the A2 for us all to relieve ourselves, presumably in full view of passing motorists.

The next thing I remember is seeing my front door. Getting my key into the keyhole was one of those classic challenges. I made a circle out of the thumb and forefinger of my left hand and placed it around the keyhole. I then successfully aimed the key into the circle and hole! Having managed that, I slammed the door and turned to face the stairs. I can still picture the cream-coloured wall at the top of the flight as I crashed into it at speed. I would never have mounted the stairs slowly without falling backwards. I turned right on the landing, undressed and slipped into bed.

'Did you have a nice time?' Ruth asked in her genuine, kind way.

I think I said that it had been surprising. As usual, I was up at seven in the morning, suited and booted and off to work as right as ninepence. Although we were always on good terms with young John and his wife, we never actually went out for another drink.

When a man who has had a little too much to drink finds himself in the street and wants to relieve himself, what is the attraction of a well-lit lamppost? Surely a dark corner makes more sense, but there I was in the full light of the lamp, when a police car stopped beside me. It was a Morris Minor 1000. The policemen did not mention what I was doing, but asked for my name, address and reason for being out at two o'clock in the morning. Satisfied with my answers, they bid me goodnight.

Five minutes later, when I was almost home, after walking for over an hour, I heard the word 'Laurence!' The same police car had pulled up beside me.

'Get in the car please; we need to take you to Gravesend.'

'I've just walked from there,' I protested, but I had to go.

'There's been a robbery and we are chasing four men, so we are picking up anyone on foot,' explained the constable, who seemed an agreeable, polite chap.

I was quite mellow when we pulled up beside a rather tough looking sergeant back in Gravesend.

'Where have you been?' he demanded.

'I had a drink with a work colleague and was walking home,' I replied, clearly and calmly.

'Oh, you do work do you?' he retorted.

Unmoved and polite, I informed him that I did work.

'Take him in!' he snapped.

'Sarge', said my constable, 'his name and address checked out and he wasn't panting when we picked him up.'

I'm jolly glad I wasn't panting! The sergeant changed his mind and the two constables drove me to my door. We actually sat chatting about cars for the next twenty minutes. Ruth and I had just bought a three year old Ford Anglia, red and white and in immaculate condition. We had recently sold a Hillman Imp and our first car had been a Morris Minor given to Ruth by her dad. Well, the police were moving from Morris Minors, which had high roofs and would accommodate a tall police helmet, to Hillman Imps as they were starting to wear flatter hats. They were also about to use Ford Anglias, so the policemen and I had plenty to talk about. Another late night. I still seem to have no problem going to bed late and getting up early, if the mood simply takes me that way.

The house two doors away from us had a very pleasant young couple living there. They both worked for a bank in London and left the house together every morning to catch the train. We socialised a little, so we were very surprised when we popped in one evening to find the lady of the house was alone. She was dividing everything from cutlery to chairs into two piles. She readily explained that they were to separate and get a divorce. That may not seem very strange nowadays, but divorce was rather rare and we had not experienced it with anyone we knew. We went home quite baffled. Married couples falling out of love was not an option that had crossed our minds.

Ruth soon transferred from her position at the Brook Hospital to the nearer Gravesend and North Kent Hospital. She was doing a very important job in her new role cross-matching blood for transfusions, but the responsibility was so high and the pay so low that again we began to look at other options. The Wellcome Foundation in Dartford offered twice the salary for what seemed to be a less responsible and stressful job. She accepted a position in their laboratories testing new drugs and various other products before they were put on the market. As this followed the disastrous thalidomide drug of the 1960s, when babies were born with deformities, it turned out to be another important role for Ruth.

One evening, coming home to Gravesend on the train, two colleagues of mine were sitting opposite an attractive young woman who was reading a book. A somewhat scruffy-looking chap sitting next to her kept falling asleep and toppling onto her shoulder, which my friends found offensive. She shrugged him off every time and he sat upright, only to nod off and slump onto her again. As the train approached his stop, one of my workmates said to the girl, 'Do you want us to sort him out? He shouldn't do that.' She replied, 'Oh no, he's my boyfriend. Come on you, this is our station.'

One minor event whilst living in our first house often enters my mind. I was at home one weekday, while Ruth was at work. I was up a ladder painting the outside window frames, in ancient times, before double glazing and UPVC. I heard a voice below calling to me, 'Is your mother in?' It was clearly a salesman.

'No,' I replied truthfully.

'Is your father in?'

'No,' I replied again, as Dad lived in Folkestone with my mother.

'Are you all on your own?'

'Yes,' I said.

'Then I'll call back another time,' he said with resignation and left.

When Ruth came home on the bus, I told her this little tale and how he must have thought that I was a teenager. Ruth informed me that she had just been charged half fare on the bus. Now that meant that the conductor took her to be no older than fourteen!

When we married in September, we had both weighed eight stone and seven pounds (yes) but by Christmas we were both eleven stone! We put this down to too much food and contentment and plunged into a diet. Within weeks, Ruth was nine stone and I was ten stone, achieved just by cutting down on things like bread and butter.

We usually went to a particular pub on a Saturday night, drank too much and had to go back for the car on Sunday morning. There were some good pubs in Gravesend and we would all enjoy listening and dancing to Tamla Motown and Reggae. Many of you will know that the success of Motown was down to Berry Gordy Junior and the great Smokey Robinson, who was a favourite of ours. We were jigging around to Smokey's songs and some Reggae one evening when a lady friend of ours, who looked very much like the young Barbara Windsor, slipped and sat on a wine glass, which broke. Blood quickly spread over her white, silky, tight-fitting dress and her curvaceous bottom. You are visualising this, aren't you? Well, she was taken to the local accident and emergency centre by her boyfriend, while we carried on dancing. We saw her next a few weeks later and, as usual, I needed to know what had transpired.

'How did it go at the hospital?' I asked.

'Well, it wasn't too bad that night when I went in. A nice elderly doctor cleaned my wound and put in some stitches. It was when I went back to have them removed that I had a bit of a shock. I don't know why, really, but I was very embarrassed. I was expecting that same nice old gentleman, for some unknown reason. You know, he was a bit like my dad, so I didn't mind, but when I went into this room to get undressed and take down my knickers, in came this tall, young West Indian chap and there I was with no pants on. He was very gentle and carefully took out the stitches, but all I could think about was his great big hands touching my little bottom!'

It's an image that I find difficult to erase, despite not being there at the time.

One evening, for my birthday treat, Ruth and I were driving into London to see a show, when we witnessed a dreadful accident. We pulled up behind another car waiting at a zebra crossing. As an old lady and two small children started to cross, another car shot round the outside of us and hit the group on the crossing. One child was knocked sideways, but was able to get up, whilst the smaller child flew through the air and landed on the pavement. He bounced, but was also unharmed. Meanwhile, the old lady was pushed about forty yards by the car and killed. She was so far from us that we could not see her clearly, but a lorry driver checked her body and put a coat over her head and shoulders. I was shocked, but somehow it did not seem real and affected me less than I expected. Police arrived and took details of everyone, including us. This was followed by a police visit to our home and a statement from us regarding what we saw. All this led to yet another one of those moments that made a lasting impression on me, when we arrived at the Old Bailey as witnesses for the prosecution. I may have thought that these elderly judges were probably past their best, but this one changed my mind. He was as sharp as a razor. The accused had changed his plea from not guilty to guilty of dangerous driving. He did this when the defence saw that the prosecution witnesses had actually turned up at court. We were not required to speak, but sat and watched as the defence pleaded mitigating circumstances. The judge did not miss a trick. He sprang to life and rightly overturned all the excuses for the driver's action. He found the chap guilty, but I was surprised that the penalty was just a three years ban and a fine.

Although I was most impressed by an apparently old judge, I was unimpressed with the layout of the courts. I did not like the experience of everyone mixing together around the corridors, whether they were the accused, the victim's loved ones or witnesses. It was also unpleasant and embarrassing to rub shoulders with the guilty party afterwards whilst he paid his fine and I was given some travel expenses.

Whilst working in the computer systems department as a business analyst, I attended a number of courses away from home. The hotel accommodation that we were allowed was not very grand in those days and we usually had to share a room with another delegate. You hoped it would be somebody you knew, but this did not always happen. I attended a particular course with a colleague Ron, who was much older than me. I am glad it was only two days, because on entering the room we saw there was only a double bed. Funnily enough for two happily married men, we seemed hardly bothered at bedtime when we popped on pyjamas, said goodnight and had a perfectly good sleep. Eric Morecambe and Ernie Wise never seemed to have a problem either and they shared a bed on television.

I must tell you about an incident at the local squash club, because it illustrated something that interests me, namely the somewhat surprising difference in ability between two people, who might at first appear to be evenly matched. Once a week I would play squash against my good friend Dave, whilst our wives chatted at Dave's house. The club had a professional coach, who was extremely good, in fact unbeaten. He was six feet tall, aged thirty-five and very athletic. You know the type. One evening, Dave and I watched an exhibition match between him and a former world champion, who was a short, rotund, ageing Pakistani named Khan. All things considered, especially Khan's age and shape, I thought it would be a close competition with our coach probably victorious. Our considerably younger club professional was sent all over the court by Khan, who rarely had to move more than a yard or two from the centre of the court or 'T'. It ended with a convincing victory for the older man and an exhausted local coach, who really was a very good player. A few minutes later I noticed him throwing up in the car park, whilst his opponent had hardly got into a sweat. I find that difference in class quite incredible at times.

We spent three years living in Gravesend and they were happy times. We had jobs, a house, fun and one another.

-8-

HOLIDAYS ABROAD…
JOINING THE 'FOREIGN LEGION'

'Come, woo me, woo me; for now I am in holiday humour,
and like enough to consent'
(As You Like It by William Shakespeare, 1600)

In 1970 Ruth and I had our first foreign holiday together on the attractive Mediterranean island of Corsica, which is a region of France. As it happened, it would also be our last vacation away from the British Isles for about twelve years. The flight to Bastia on the north of the island was the first of more than 130 trips I would make overseas by plane. Ruth had flown before as a child and was fine, but I was a little apprehensive. Overall, I enjoyed the new experience, despite being amazed at how a big heavy plane can actually take off and fly. A rather rickety old coach took us down the coast at high speed to the capital Ajaccio, where we were staying. As the road was both bumpy and very close to sheer drops into the sea, I arrived feeling sick and somewhat unsettled. I soon recovered my composure and on our first evening we went for a relaxing walk. As we strolled in that warm air, scented by the local wild plants, we met two Foreign Legionnaires, who were both English and based on the island. The Legion is a unit of the French Army and they were awaiting their next assignment. The two soldiers overheard us speaking and introduced themselves. They were very friendly and explained that they had both been on the run from the British authorities, until they had met at a police station in Paris, where they joined the Legion. This was how it was done apparently. One was a Londoner, who had been a member of the infamous Jack Spot's gang and was wanted for violence. He seemed very interested in the problems the Krays were having at the time. In appearance he was short and stocky, the image of that fine British actor Bob Hoskins. The other chap, a bank robber, was from Manchester and somewhat taller than his friend. He reminded me very much of Eric Morecambe. No offence to those two admirable stars of our television screens.

They seemed to like us and, slightly worryingly, they joined us at our hotel for an evening meal. They clearly commanded huge respect or fear from the restaurant staff. Their meals appeared to be first class and free. The service they received was the most attentive imaginable, almost grovelling. I was simply interested in their stories, but I also thought it wise to be friendly, as there was a certain aura about them! They said goodnight and told us they would be on the beach the next day and to watch out for them landing by parachute, so we said we would.

I had actually forgotten about our new 'friends' when we were lying on the sunny sands the following morning. Just then a small plane went over and a dozen or so paratroopers emerged. They floated gently downwards, but did not land near us, so I thought no more of it. A little later, Ruth and I were wading in the warm, shallow sea with sardines swimming around our legs, when suddenly up popped some frogmen with face masks, snorkels and a cheery, 'Hello, did you see us?' 'Well, yes,' I replied. 'What have you got there?' Our two chaps and a red-headed Scottish colleague of theirs held up some black slippery stingray they had caught for lunch. They were carefully cutting off the stinging portions and tying the rays to their belts. They insisted that we join them for food and drinks a little further along the beach. We thought it would be interesting and agreed to the idea.

Lunch was barbecued stingray accompanied by the cheapest red wine imaginable. Then the real stories started. Their particular regiment consisted of a few English, a few more Scots, no French and the vast majority German. They had recently returned from being loaned out to various other armies fighting around the world. Our chaps pointed out two well-built colleagues in skimpy black swimming trunks strutting along the beach. Apparently, they had been seen happily slitting the throats of women and children in African villages. They also mentioned that one of their colleagues was no longer with them, literally, as he had killed the commanding officer's pet sheep. The CO was not amused and it would be gratuitous for me to describe what they said happened to the sheep-killer, but his remains were buried on the island.

You can meet some unusual people on holiday, but these two were a bit much and we were really quite glad not to run into them again. We loved the island and were amazed to find that whilst the temperature was about 95F on the beach, we could immediately drive up through snow-covered mountains. One evening we sat with a drink, halfway up the mountain and saw the fastest and one of the loveliest sunsets we have ever seen. The fierce red sun just dropped out of the sky.

A year earlier, in 1969, we had taken the car ferry from Fishguard in Wales to Rosslare, County Wexford in the Republic of Ireland. We had been warned of a rough crossing, but it was surprisingly smooth and we drove straight to a bar for some legendary Guinness. The barman was celebrating his twenty-first birthday and the birth of his third child, so the drink was flowing. So much so that everyone was blind drunk and you had to serve yourself. Money was left on the bar, swimming in spilt alcohol. They must have liked us, as it was closing time and they locked the door with us inside! Fine fellows kept giving me drinks and telling me that Larry was an Irish name, so we could stay as long as we liked.

At one point there was a loud knock on the door, but luckily it was only the police coming in for a drink. The door was locked again behind them and a good night was had by all. I do not remember sleeping, but the next day we drove to Blarney Castle, near Cork, to kiss the Blarney Stone. It is supposed to give you eloquence or 'the gift of the gab', so hopefully it has helped my story-telling. You be the judge.

A few days later, on 21st July we were staying in the pretty town of Killarney in County Kerry. We soon became aware that morning that a number of small boats had American Stars and Stripes flags raised and numerous empty champagne bottles aboard. The previous day had been momentous in history when Neil Armstrong became the first man to walk on the Moon. The astronaut stepped onto the Moon's surface after first opening the hatch on the Eagle landing craft. He had earlier reported, 'Houston, Tranquility Base here. The Eagle has landed.' Armstrong then declared: 'That's one small step for man, one giant leap for mankind.' The Americans were certainly celebrating!

Remember this is Ireland. Well it is the only time that I have ever had sunstroke and it is horrendous. It was a glorious, golden, sunny beach with what turned out to be a deceptive breeze. I had sunscreen and towels over most of me, as we could tell that the sun was fairly hot. Ruth had just the sunscreen. We left the beach a little burned, but it was not until we were in the bar in the early evening that the full horror struck. I had to have a glass of beer removed from my hand as I started to shake uncontrollably. Ruth, who had no ill-effects from the sun, guided me to our room, carefully removed my clothes and smothered me in a cool lotion, which melted on contact. I was glowing bright red. I slept a little, but I was shaking and feeling sick all night. My head was thumping and for the only time in my life I believe I was hallucinating and wanted to die. The worst was over by morning except for the pain involved in moving every burnt joint in my body. After more lotion, I got dressed with help, but every movement for two days was very painful. I would not have guessed that burning your ankles would make trying to walk hurt so much. It has never happened again, probably because I never actually sunbathe. Fortunately, I manage to pick up a healthy tan just being outdoors.

Due to the fact that we had young children, about whom I will tell you a lot more later, we did not bother to go abroad again until 1982. This was when we did our 'grand tour' of the USA and Canada over a period of four weeks. Although our son Clive was only ten and our daughter Kate only eight at the time, they still clearly remember visiting New York and seeing the truly magnificent and moving Statue of Liberty for the first time. I could immediately imagine how the many immigrants to the United States felt so full of hope as it came into view. Ruth, the children and I climbed right up inside the structure and looked out through the crown. It was hot and quite a squeeze. As I had already seen the Eiffel Tower in Paris, it was obvious that the internal iron structure of this iconic siren was designed and engineered by the same man, Gustave Eiffel. The monument was officially titled Liberty Enlightening the World and was presented by the people of France to the USA in 1886 to commemorate its centennial. The crown of the statue was subsequently closed to the public in 1984 for a major renovation, so it was fortunate that we visited it two years earlier. Following the destruction of the Twin Towers of the World Trade Center in September 2001, the entire statue was closed. It was finally reopened on 4th July 2009. However, it still had the same problem of a tight spiral staircase up to the crown, the top of which was 20 degrees Fahrenheit hotter than at ground level. After New York, we spent two weeks in California and I will tell you a little about that in my next chapter. Then we flew to Canada, where we had a couple of delightfully mad friends, Marje and John, from my university days. They had emigrated from Kent to join her parents, who were living in Calgary. Ruth, the kids and I joined them in a 'recreational vehicle' journey from her mum and dad's home in Calgary, through the Rockies to Marje and John's superb new bungalow beside the river in Kamloops. Harry the dog accompanied us on the trip, so what with their two daughters as well, the van was full. There was a North American Indian reservation across the river from their home and we all shared the clear, fast-flowing waterway for canoeing. It was really idyllic and we had a great time with some wonderful outdoor experiences for the kids. Whilst in Canada we flew to Toronto to visit Ruth's cousin Michael and wife Maureen, making our first visit to Niagara Falls. It was a great holiday.

Ruth and I sometimes took Clive's friend Paul abroad with us and Kate. Paul was an only child and his young dad was confined to a wheelchair. It was just as well that I enjoyed kicking a ball about, going down water chutes and having a bit of rough and tumble, which I think was good for Paul. One year we all went to Spain, which is unusual for us, but just right for the kids at that time. Sun, beach, water and fun were the order of the day. I don't know how this started, but sometimes in the evenings we would act out well-known stories like Little Red Riding Hood or Snow White just for fun. Quite often we each had several parts and Clive captured it on his video camera, as well as having to play, say, the Big Bad Wolf. Our attempts at acting more than one part in the same scene were hilarious. I had not laughed so much since I was a boy, when we would tumble onto the floor in hysterics, holding our chests in pain and wheezing with laughter.

Obviously we tried to take good care of Paul on these trips, except that he was nearly killed three times during the Spanish holiday. The worst incident was horse-riding, which we did most years. The organizers appeared to be children and 'health and safety' had not been invented, but we felt committed to the ride and thought it would be OK. As the trek started we were warned that two of our horses did not like one another and should be kept apart. Also, one of the horses was a bit wild and another liked to bite anything that got too close. Apart from that, it would be fine. Within a few minutes, Clive and Paul's horses were spooked and bolted for the woods. I sat in horror as first Clive was knocked clean off his mount by an overhanging branch, just like in the westerns on television. He bounced and got up unharmed, but Paul's horse stopped so suddenly that he flew over its head and nose-dived into the ground. I assumed at least a broken neck from a fall like that. I was also fairly sure that I had killed a friend's only child. Remarkably, he was absolutely fine and I have rarely felt so relieved about anything, but I still cannot see how he escaped serious injury. The next day, whilst larking about with me, he disappeared over a steep slope and it was chiefly my fault. With my heart in my mouth, I looked over the edge and he was scrambling back up, again unharmed. Next it was the go-carts, which the boys loved. Again there was no health and safety in evidence, but not much could go wrong or so I thought. After a few laps we noticed that Paul's engine was on fire and so was his jacket. In the excitement of dueling with Clive, he had not yet become aware of the flames, until we frantically attracted his attention. He managed to stop the vehicle and very quickly removed the burning garment. Once again he escaped unharmed and a new jacket was purchased.

In April 1987, as part of my fortieth birthday celebrations, family Brooks took a car ferry across the channel to Holland. We drove to Amsterdam and, among other activities, we visited the Anne Frank Museum for the first time. We all found it very moving. As I have this tendency to repeat things many years later, Ruth and I took Clive's two children, Emily and Scott to that museum in 2008. I mention this first trip in 1987 because, on the return journey, our boat from Vlissingen hugged the Dutch coast until it reached Zeebrugge in Belgium in order to cross back to England. As we left Zeebrugge, my eagle-eye son spotted the unfortunate ferry ship MS Herald of Free Enterprise. We were well aware of the dreadful tragedy that occurred on the night of 6th March, when it capsized moments after leaving port. It was a roll-on roll-off (RORO) car and passenger ferry owned by Townsend Thoresen. That night 193 passengers and crew were killed, making this the worst maritime disaster in peacetime involving a British registered ship since 1919. There was a successful operation to refloat the ship in late April 1987 and there it was in front of us as we returned to England.

We had a slightly ridiculous incident on a trip to Florida with Clive and Kate, also in 1987. We were driving through Miami on a very hot day, when we spotted (or rather Clive spotted) an establishment that gave water-skiing lessons, so we screeched to a halt. It was $22 for five journeys on the skis around the bay, the last two of which would be solo. It was an expensive little stop, but we wanted our kids to experience everything they had the courage to attempt. I queued on a boardwalk clutching a $20 bill and two $1 bills for the ticket. In front of me was a huge German chap, who was wearing khaki shorts over his large round bottom. A big bundle of dollar bills were poking dangerously out of his back pocket and as he stepped forward, the whole lot flew from the pocket onto the pathway in front of me. I instantly pounced on the valuable wad to prevent it going in the water. As I stood up, he spun round and angrily grabbed them from me, calling me a thief. Unfortunately, he had my three notes too! I tried to explain what had happened and about my $22, but he was ranting furiously in German and would not try to understand. Despite his red face and massive bulk, I stood my ground, as I seriously needed my money back. I was rescued by the proprietor, who asked, 'What's up, buddy?' I told him very simply what had happened, with actions, and he understood immediately. I said that at the top of the German's wad he would find a measly $22 of mine. He explained this in English, which had not worked for me, to the slightly calmer German, who then studied his money with interest. He stared at the $22 for a while, then at me, and then came a massive apology. 'You saved my money and this is your money' he said. 'I'm so sorry, I apologize'. He smiled, shook my hand vigorously and turned out to be a very pleasant fellow. Unfortunately, I could not get rid of him. I simply wanted to stand with Ruth and Kate in order to watch Clive, but he followed me around, continuously patting my back, shaking my hand and apologizing. I suppose I had prevented several hundred dollars going into the water, but I wished he would just watch his daughter ski, while I watched Clive.

One unusual trip that I took with my son was to Poland in October 1989. Clive was seventeen years old and we travelled by coach with around sixty other football fans to see England play Poland. The venue was the Slaski Stadium, which lies between Chorzow and Katowice. The outward journey was via France, Belgium, Holland, West Germany and East Germany. It was fairly uneventful except for two incidents. First, Clive decided to open a tin of food on the coach. This was a special can that heated up the food inside, when you activate it by pulling a ring. The thing almost exploded with an outpouring of smelly gas that filled most of the coach. Very embarrassing, but the meal was tasty, apparently. We opened another one in the middle of a park, behind some bushes, but the explosive noise was still rather too audible. What with the smoke as well, we were lucky that the police didn't take an interest. The second incident was the crossing of Checkpoint Alpha and a section of no man's land between West and East Germany. The mood of the border guards was solemn and somewhat menacing. They took as long as possible to check our passports and we were delayed several hours, before being allowed to continue. Little were we to know that within a month the Berlin Wall would be torn down after twenty-eight years of division and this would lead to the unification of Germany in October 1990. As East and West Germany both had good football teams and strong traditions in athletics, I remember thinking how powerful a combined country would be at sport, but I don't believe that turned out to be the case at all.

Before we reached the football stadium, we stopped for a drink in a Polish bar. It was unforgettable. For a start, the beer was less than 2p per pint, so I bought the whole coach party a drink for under a pound. The publican had never had so many customers before and resorted to old glasses under the bar. He obviously did not stop to wash them, as some contained dirt and spiders' webs. When some chaps ordered a second pint, the price had risen to 3p per pint, which my son puts down to market forces! The beer was pretty poor anyway and a lot was left in the mugs, especially when the debris was spotted. Later, we stopped for a wash at a hotel, as we had slept on the coach. I noticed that the room rate was the equivalent of only one pound sterling per night and it was a perfectly respectable hotel. I popped in the gift shop, but it was almost bare except for a tiny plastic doll in a cot. We briefly looked in the high street, but the only non-food shop with anything for sale had just two briefcases on display. It seemed very stark and sad.

When we reached the ground, we were surrounded by Polish boys wanting to swap anything they had for football mementos. They were pleasant young lads, dressed in anoraks and jeans, just like our boys, but they had practically nothing to offer in exchange. I remember their fresh hopeful faces, as they gathered round us. My fellow travellers gave them what they could and I wished we had taken more things with us to hand out. Even the young soldiers on duty inside the ground wanted to swap their army badges for football badges and some did.

A few Polish fans traded Solidarity badges with our coach party. This was the non-communist trade union that by August 1989 led the coalition government. In December that year Lech Walesa, their union leader, was elected President of Poland. This was an amazing turn of events in my view and he seemed to be a very brave man.

Incidentally, the game ended in a goalless draw with Peter Shilton, in goal for England, making four fine saves, according to my diary, and Poland hitting our bar in injury time!

Coincidentally, as I write this story in April 2009, Ruth and I have just returned from a united Berlin, where we spent five very happy days with our two eldest grandchildren. We stayed in a smart hotel near Checkpoint

Charlie. You may know that the checkpoints were named after the NATO Phonetic Alphabet, hence Alpha and Charlie.

In 1992, after many years apart, I met up again with my dad's younger brother Bob, still living in Muswell Hill, north London. We got onto the subject of holidays and I told him that Ruth and I were going to Hong Kong in October. Well, he then told me that he had business interests all over the world, which rather surprised me, and visited Hong Kong several times a year, including the coming October. By coincidence, it turned out that he would be there at exactly the same time as us. He said that he should turn up at 'his company' and ask for him or one of his joint MDs. We did this in October and found it was a toy exporting business with factories over the border in China. We were treated royally by Bob, his two London-born MDs and their Hong Kong Chinese wives. We could not have had a better time, what with personal guides and lavish meals. Bob was a big, dark-haired, rather abrupt man, who was obviously tough in business situations, but was very kind and generous to us. Slightly shocking, on our way into China to see the factory, was the sight of kittens for sale in the street food market. Also rather obvious was the lack of development of China, just yards across the border from the highly modern Hong Kong. Chinese road builders and labourers were dressed in light clothing, sandals and wide-brimmed hats to shield them from the sun. There were no safety helmets or boots in evidence and they were using no mechanical aids. They had large, wide shovels to lay out a new road and their materials were loaded on horse-drawn carts with the rather bored-looking animals waiting to edge slowly forward, as work progressed. During our evening meals Bob's assistants and wives told us that they were concerned by what might happen when Hong Kong was handed back to the People's Republic of China in 1997 and five million residents would lose British citizenship. They had already bought properties in Australia, where their children were at school, just in case they felt obliged to move on. Chris Patten, the former Chairman of the Conservative Party, was appointed as the last Governor of Hong Kong in June 1992 and by all accounts was very popular. Our hotel overlooked his residence, so it was all most interesting for us. Mr Patten did ensure a smooth handover and I believe that things went much better than expected for companies such as Bob's, by which time he had passed away at home in north London.

In 1993, Ruth and I decided on a camping holiday in the south of France with another couple, Mick and Gill. The site was terraced, so that there were a few tents above our row and some below. You had a pitch wide enough to drive your car up to the plot and erect your canvas, which we did successfully. All was well, until we heard the family above us. They were British and very loud. They also seemed to be permanently angry with one another. We had a very pleasant Danish couple in the adjacent tent and they spoke beautiful, clear English. We were not proud to admit that we were from the same country as the noisy group above. First there was the wife constantly screaming the names of the husband and son, who were always doing something of which she disapproved. I do not really blame her, but her voice was piercing. Secondly, her rather dull hubby was always fiddling with the car and moving it backwards and forwards above our heads, sometimes revving the engine before studying something under the bonnet. The wife became quite incensed when the fool let the car roll into their tent. Despite doing little damage, it frightened all of us. They also erected a complicated, stringed arrangement for all their pots and pans to hang from in a narrow walkway above our tent. Their lad was always squeezing past it and being screamed at to be careful, until one day when he knocked the whole lot down onto us. Yet again, there was much shrieking from mother. Probably to take our minds off their unpleasant voices and our general nervousness in being below them, we all drank rather a lot of wine one evening. Consequently, Gill needed to empty her bladder and, as it was rather late and a bit too dark to walk to the toilet, we allowed her to use a bucket in a separate little area of the tent. Unfortunately, her action made a great deal of obvious noise, so we started to sing to mask the sound. Imagine our surprise when a horrid female voice from above bellowed, 'Shut up or we'll report you to the concierge!'

In 1994, we drove to the south of France to visit some friends, John and Pauline, who had decided to live there. We cannot be satisfied with a single purpose for a journey, so we decided to look for the battlefields of Crecy and Agincourt en route. Crecy was easy to find. The battle had taken place in August 1346, when a much smaller English army commanded by Edward III, who happily turns out to be an ancestor of mine, defeated Philip VI of France. Much of the success was attributed to the use of the longbow. The French armoured knights wore chain mail and plate, but this was penetrated by the English arrows, before they could reach our bowmen and engage them. In the battle, the French knights and their horses were already exhausted by trying to gallop through miles of mud and were simply cut down. The French were employing Genoese crossbowmen at the front of their army, but their bolts would not reach the English as the rain slackened their crossbow strings. Our old enemy did not seem to learn much, as nearly seventy years later it happened again, at Agincourt.

Until we found the village, we did not know that, in France, it was spelt Azincourt. Still, I was delighted, as Henry V is my favourite work of Shakespeare and the play revolves around the battle at Agincourt. The date of the conflict was 25th October 1415, St Crispin's Day, as Henry reminds us in one of his great speeches. Once again, our longbowmen took out the opposing cavalry and many who sank in the mud are still there apparently buried in the field by the crossroads, where we parked our car. Ruth and I entered the little corner restaurant, which doubled as a visitor centre, and were surprised to find that it was owned and run by a very welcoming English family. They kindly allowed me to put on some chain mail and fire five arrows over the battlefield using a traditional English longbow, which I prefer to any modern bow. I said I had done some archery, but they were surprised at how well the arrows flew across that historic landscape. They went so far that the young lady said she would have to fetch them later. It was great. You may know that Shakespeare wrote for Henry V that great line, 'We few, we happy few, we band of brothers.' It was stirring stuff.

Do you remember our friends Marje and John who emigrated to Canada? Well, in 1996 they were on the move again. They travelled the world, leaving two grown up daughters in Canada, and ended up selecting the island of Dominica to be their next home. We only found out about this when they knocked on our door in Kent one day. 'Hello', I said, not entirely surprised. 'I thought you lived in Canada.' It was good to see them. They were in England seeking documents, like a copy of their marriage certificate, in order to live in Dominica. They stayed a couple of nights and we promised to visit them in their new home, when they had built it.

It was a few years later in 1999 that we had an email from Marje inviting us to stay with them, but we never need to be asked twice. We immediately flew to what is officially the Commonwealth of Dominica, an English-speaking island nation formerly owned by Britain. It has been nicknamed the "Nature Isle of the Caribbean" due to its natural beauty. During our two weeks stay, we saw everything from the lush rainforests with parrots and iguana, to the extensive banana plantations around the island. One hot, humid day we cooled off by snorkelling in the clear, shallow water where the Caribbean Sea meets the Atlantic Ocean and saw the most exotic tropical fish. During our stay, we were also very pleased to visit the shops, markets and the homes of Marje and John's many friends. Most of the 70,000 or so inhabitants are descended from African slaves, emancipated by Britain in 1834. France had formally ceded possession of Dominica to the United Kingdom in 1763, but it was not until 1978 that it became an independent nation.

Marje and John had built their large wooden bungalow themselves in a town called Portsmouth and relied on a friendly neighbour, on higher land, for their water supply. It was filtered in their loft and was freezing cold. They did not heat it and we had to get used to cold showers. These were frequent because it was so hot and humid and it soothed the insect bites. The giant ants were the worst and we did our best to keep them at bay with insect repellents. Every night we slept under those lacy white nets that keep the little critters in their place. Most days Marje would check the news for any nearby hurricanes. The house was built to resist them to an extent, but there was also a shelter down the road, which they had used a few times. The bungalow windows were always open to let air through, plus the occasional humming bird. Their garden included banana plants, mango trees and star fruits, so it was pick-your-own, which I enjoyed very much. The capital of the island is called Roseau and Marje took us there one day. The roads are very badly maintained and she could not risk their old car, so we caught the bus. This poor old vehicle officially held twelve passengers and was full by the second stop, with the three of us on board. It was then diverted to Portsmouth hospital, which I gather had rather rudimentary facilities, to pick up a patient who needed attention at the main hospital in Roseau. To my amazement, our driver took on three more customers, all standing, before arriving at the hospital. I did wonder what we were going to do with the patient, but after a while we left without him. Within five minutes we had picked up six or seven more travellers and I had a little boy on my lap. He sat perfectly still and did not speak for what was quite a long and bumpy journey. I tried making conversation, but he was shy. There are no pavements, white lines or roundabouts on the island, except a small area of pavement by the shops in Roseau. Apparently they now have one set of traffic lights somewhere. You just pull up in your vehicle wherever you fancy. If you are in the way, nobody seems bothered. Regarding John's old banger, there were 'mechanics' in Portsmouth, but they knew little about cars. John's daughters sent him spare parts from Canada and John advised the lads in the garage how to fit them. He would have done the work himself, but he was developing health problems and needed an operation. This eventually led to them leaving Dominica for Canada, permanently I assume, but you can never be sure with them. As an aside, I tried my usual thing of going for a jog around Portsmouth, but it was literally impossible. Although I can run 26 miles, I could barely complete 26 yards in that humidity. As another aside, it had been Marje and John who told us about the new-fangled credit card in the late 1960's. It was introduced in 1966 and they had one before I had heard of them. Useful as long as you do your best to pay them off. It was also those two who had persuaded us back in 1974 to take our toddler and six week old baby on a narrow boat trip up the Grand Union Canal. We were so tired working the locks every day that one evening the four adults all fell asleep with our heads in our dinner plates!

Ruth usually initiated and planned our holidays, but for our pearl anniversary in 1998, I asked to be put in sole charge. I decided to take her to Japan and keep it as a complete surprise for as long as possible. I think she was a little concerned about my choice of destination and my competence, as it was my first attempt at organising a trip of this importance. I visited an excellent travel company in London. They specialised in holidays to Japan and we arranged a few days in Tokyo, followed by a similar length of stay in Kyoto, the old capital. As I expected from an enthusiast like Ruth, she loved the idea. The holiday started brilliantly with an upgrade to first class on the plane, complete with free champagne. I had simply told a stewardess that it was the thirtieth anniversary of our wedding and that is what we got. Tokyo was most interesting and good fun. Whilst there, we discovered that they had a Disneyland, so we just had to fit it into our schedule. I am sure that it was little known outside Japan, as we saw no more than six other tourists all day. We later went to the zoo, which was also more or less free from holidaymakers. The main visitors were the many delightful parties of tiny schoolchildren, all in their brightly coloured uniforms and behaving superbly. Leaving Tokyo, we enjoyed the ride on the 'bullet train' to Kyoto and were just able to see Mount Fuji through the mist. Overall, my one and only attempt at organising our holiday was a complete success, as are all of Ruth's.

Over the years, we have embarked on several holidays driving around eastern or western Europe, mostly to experience their scenery and culture. In the year 2000, we visited a number of countries, including Germany and Switzerland, and experienced some very interesting venues. In Germany, we were quite intrigued by the engineering feat to build the 'Eagle's Nest'. This was a tea-house built in 1938 for Adolf Hitler's fiftieth birthday. It is perched on a mountain summit in the German Alps near Berchtesgaten and it is where Hitler entertained visitors. The view is great and fortunately there is still a tea room. We moved on to Murren in Switzerland and had a meal in the revolving restaurant known as Piz Gloria on the Schilthorn Mountain. This restaurant originated in Ian Fleming's James Bond novel 'On Her Majesty's Secret Service', where it was the hideout of the infamous villain, Blofeld. The film production team found the building partly constructed and financially contributed to its completion in return for filming rights.

Scotland is not really 'abroad', but I have been there many times. An outstanding memory of a visit to the Orkney Islands in 2004 is the tiny village of Skara Brae, a group of eight Neolithic dwellings dating from between 3200BC and 2200BC. It is amongst Orkney's most-visited sites and regarded by many as one of the most remarkable monuments in Europe. Considering its age, the facilities it offered, like bedrooms, toilets, fireplaces, shelved dressers and even covered ways connecting the houses was astonishing. I did not realise that Britain had something of that age and sophistication. It must have been a special place, because Adam Hart-Davis of television fame was walking around the site in front of us inspecting the ancient lavatory.

Another more recent foreign holiday with a strange occurrence was in the year 2007. Ruth and I went to Istanbul in Turkey for a few days to see where Europe met Asia. Despite the heat, we enjoyed it very much until one particular incident. The official, numbered taxis all lined up outside the major sights, so we went to jump in one. As we did so, another driver quickly ushered us into his cab instead, but we assumed that was part of the queuing system. It was a proper liveried, numbered cab, but we were surprised by the speed that he took off and the reckless way that he drove down the middle of the road, overtaking most of the traffic. He seemed quite jolly and we just hoped that he knew what he was doing. He said he had to drop us on a link road, close to our destination, because he was not allowed to drive his cab into the area we requested. That seemed okay, apart from having to walk a bit further in the heat. Then came the problem. I was expecting him to charge about seven Euros for a trip similar in length to several we had taken before. He asked for thirty-five Euros. I protested and he turned very nasty and said he would drive us back. Ruth thought he might be really dangerous and perhaps have a knife, so I agreed to pay up. As I got out my cash, he grabbed the lot, jumped in his cab and took off, leaving us on the pavement. I must say that I was very surprised, as nothing like this had ever happened to me before in any of the forty or more countries that I had visited. He had taken about sixty Euros, so I decided to report this to the police. Annoyed and slightly shaken, we walked in the heat towards the place we wanted to visit and soon spotted a policeman along the route. He did not know any English, but found a shopkeeper who explained that we should walk up the road to the police station. In there, a very polite and sympathetic young woman with an excellent command of English took the details, including the number of the cab, which I had written down. Then, unfortunately, she informed me that where the incident took place was outside her area, which must be rather small, and I would have to walk to another police station to report it again. Well, it was far too hot to do that, so we left it. They were trying to help and apologized on behalf of Istanbul for what had happened to us, but their system for putting it right needs to improve. Despite my elaborating on this incident, we shrugged it off and enjoyed the rest of our visit. It was great to see their architecture, experience their culture and to take a leisurely river boat trip up the Bosphorus, which is the strait separating the European and Asian parts of Turkey. We do love history and geography!

Living in Kent, the Eurotunnel car shuttle is very convenient for us. Since it was opened in 1994 by Queen Elizabeth II and President Mitterrand, we have used it many times, always driving on and off in England and France without incident. It was not, however, the same for a friend of mine. Having spent two weeks driving around France, Steve and family arrived back at Calais for the trip home. He was early and when the train came in, he was third in the queue. The leading British cars were beckoned onto the train, so Steve followed. They were waved through the compartments for quite some time until they eventually drove off the train under the guidance of a member of staff. A little puzzled, they stopped in a line and got out to ask what was happening. There were just seven cars on this patch of tarmac and the door of the carriage they had just left was now closed behind them. The staff had disappeared, so Steve and one other chap ran off to find someone. They did locate some employees of Eurotunnel, but could not make it clear, due to the language barrier, that they were trying to go to England and had been at the front of the queue. It was assumed by the French that they had just arrived from England. Even when an English-speaking official was found, they had quite a job explaining what had happened. They were told to go to the back of the queue and got very angry, again trying to point out that they were originally first in that line! When the penny dropped, the official apologized and led them to the front of the queue to board the train, only for the magnificent seven to be booed by holidaymakers who thought they had been given a special privilege to jump the queue!

Whilst on holiday, I often indulge in one of my favourite pastimes of chatting to people and finding those amazing coincidences that link us together. I call it serendipity. A very good example was when Ruth and I were wandering around the Sphinx and Pyramids in Cairo, Egypt. We started speaking to another couple, as you do, and made some connections. She was from Southgate, north London, like Ruth, and went to Kingston University, like our son Clive. He was from Gillingham in Kent, where we live now, and went to the same school as Clive, where Ruth was also a laboratory technician. We asked his surname, which was Sheepshanks, and he told us that he was a general practitioner in a village some thirty miles from Gillingham. We realized from the unusual surname that his elderly parents lived very close to us and so the conversation developed. A few weeks later some friends came to dinner and we were telling them about our holiday. When we got to the coincidence about the Sheepshanks, our friends said 'Oh, he's our doctor!'

Here's a bit of serendipity-style madness with a holiday connection for you. Bear with me while I explain. My brother Gordon and I were always as different as Del and Rodney Trotter in the classic sitcom Only Fools and Horses. He is nine years older than me and three inches shorter. His hair is brown, whilst mine is black, turning grey. Our eyes and noses are not alike and I am told we speak differently. Now, I used to visit an old pal named Doug and very occasionally I would briefly overlap with a lady named Margaret, who was another old friend of his. One day, I was at Doug's and he informed me that Margaret had met Gordon, who was a complete stranger to her, on holiday in Spain. I rang my brother and asked him how this came about. His reply stunned me and every friend and relation that knows us both. Apparently, she walked up to him and asked whether he had a brother named Larry in England. He confirmed it and they got on very well, but he and his wife Carina had no explanation as to how Margaret managed this deduction. Intrigued, I rang Margaret as soon as possible and her husband Trevor answered the telephone. He believed that Margaret had recognized Gordon's laugh or the way he walked and decided that, although we were completely unalike in appearance, he must be my brother!

In July 2005, Ruth and I agreed with my Newcastle-supporting friend, Michael, to a secret plan to surprise his wife Julie on her fortieth birthday, in Rome. She thought they were going with just two other pals from the north-east. I used one of these folk, who secretly informed Michael, to exchange messages and synchronize our shock visit to Michael and Julie's hotel room. It was to be at 8.20am precisely on the day of her birthday, carrying a celebratory cake alight with candles. We were in the same corridor just a few doors away from them, unknown to Julie. Exciting, isn't it? Ruth had brought a chocolate cake and candles in our luggage and I popped out early to buy some matches, in Italian! I stood there in the shop demonstrating the striking of a match, which they kindly understood. At 8.15am Ruth was keen to light the candles and do the deed, but I knew it had to be done at exactly 8.20am, so that Michael could be prepared for us. Within a few minutes, with a flaming cake, I knocked. There was some delay, as we were later informed that Michael insisted on Julie opening the door, despite her being in a dressing gown and curlers. As I said, 'Rooma servicea', in my best Italian, her face was a mixture of total shock and pleasure. During hugs and kisses, after blowing out the candles, she shakily asked what we were doing in Rome. Giving her no chance to recover her composure, I explained that the Pope had requested an audience with me and as we were in the area, we thought we would look her up. After two days of fun, delicious meals and sight-seeing, we flew back to England, pleased with the whole plan, as was Julie.

I am now going to leap forward to 2009, when I wrote 99% of this book, and summarize this year's main holidays and events, as this is rapidly becoming a travelogue. Actually, writing one of those is another suggestion often made to Ruth and me! Apart from taking Em and Scott to Berlin in April, Ruth and I drove around France, Spain and Portugal for two weeks in July to celebrate her retirement. Much as she had enjoyed her job and workmates, it was great for her to get away from it all. We also went to Wales for the wedding of our friends Rod and Daph's son Alex to a Liverpudlian lass named Liz. We last saw Rod and Daph in their home in Sweden ten years ago, but it seemed just like yesterday, and that's friendship for you. We then had a really nice week in Centerparcs with my daughter and family, whom I will introduce to you as soon as possible. Our 'slightly mad friends' Marje and John, who now live in Canada again, popped in to see us for the night in early November as part of their European tour. This is despite John being three years into multiple sclerosis and Marje recovering from breast cancer. Finally, in 2009, we have just spent a week in Brazil followed by another week in the Falkland Islands. We started in Rio de Janeiro, where the highlights were the magnificent Statue of Christ, the miles of hot, sandy beach in Copacabana and Ipanema and the gorgeous Botanical Gardens with toucans flying in from the adjacent Atlantic rain forest. Even better were the Iguassu Falls, also in Brazil. This wonderful waterfall is the largest in the world and more stunning than I could possibly describe. Although it is only eighty-three meters high (compared to the 900 meters of Angel Falls in Venezuela) it is 2.3 kilometers wide and the effect of this massive volume of water is unbelievable unless you see it. We also walked through a rain forest full of wildlife to see the falls from the Argentinian side, which is even better. I have seen some natural phenomena in my time and this is one of the best. The beautiful area is enhanced by clouds of huge butterflies of every colour, but my favourites were the brilliant yellow and orange ones that landed on your clothes. Due to the heat and humidity, we were perspiring, so the butterflies landed on our moist arms and we could feel them probing amongst the salty sweat. We saw dark brown capuchin monkeys complete with babies clinging on for dear life as they swept through the trees. There were also 'big lizards', ring-tailed coatimundi raccoons and the cheery little 'good-to-see-you' birds. Wonderful.

We were probably even more thrilled by the Falklands, where we toured the battlefields around Port Stanley, visiting such famous sites as San Carlos, Goose Green and Darwin. We also saw the ancient grave and memorial to my great-great-great-great grandfather Robert Dyer at the Old Settlement on Saunders Island. It was magical to see and sit among penguins, elephant seals and albatrosses. I kept going back to the Rockhoppers for another look, as they were so cute and friendly. We even watched killer whales hunting for young seals, which we saw again at exactly the same venue, but on the television programme Life two weeks later, narrated by the great naturalist Sir David Attenborough. Anyway, it was all absolutely fantastic and I will be telling you more about Robert Dyer later. I sincerely thank all the people we met for their hospitality, especially Susan and David Pole-Evans, who own Saunders. The Falklanders are very British and must remain so, without question.

As I mentioned earlier, I have flown more than 130 times, so I would like to end this chapter by telling you about one of the best flights Ruth and I have ever had. It was a trip to Lapland with our daughter-in-law Victoria and our two eldest grandchildren. This was in December 2005 and we were going, of course, to see the real Father Christmas. The children, Emily and Scott, were told that they were simply waving goodbye to me and Ruth, as we took a trip abroad. They did not know until we had collected the boarding cards that we were going to Lapland and that they were coming too. I have never seen them so thrilled by anything. They jumped on their mother, laughed, cried and looked so excited that it was very moving. The airplane was full of the most polite and pleasant children who were given imitation reindeer horns to wear and even had space to play games. The pilot told them that he needed help to land the plane, which meant that they must stamp their feet and cheer. The trip was very surprising and quite fantastic. The landing in Lapland was the prettiest sight with snow-covered conifers and paths lit by flaming drums of oil. We patted reindeer and took a husky-drawn sledge through the forest to Santa's log cabin, which was idyllic. We were shown in by 'elves' and there was the best grotto and Santa that you could imagine. Poor little Scott had lost the list of presents he wanted, but by some miracle Father Christmas gave him the toy at the top of his list. We were amazed and the kids were absolutely in awe.

So, you see that our foreign holidays give us much education and great pleasure. They will continue whilst we remain fit and well enough to travel.

-9-

CHILDREN …
'AS YOU SOW SO SHALL YOU REAP'

'The old fashioned respect for the young is fast dying out'
(Oscar Wilde, 1895)

'What are you doing?' I anxiously asked the junior midwife. It was February 1974 and my second child was about to be born, but so far only her head was out in the wide world. Suddenly, this young lady grabbed two clamps and attached them somewhere between the baby's head and my wife. I knew that this was only her third delivery and I was rather concerned at what she was doing. After all, I had seen my son born two years earlier, when the clamps were attached to the umbilical and the cord cut only when he had fully emerged, so I thought that this young lady's action might be wrong. 'Cord round neck,' she said in broken English, 'but my other two babies were cord round neck also, so I know what to do.' How lucky we were to have her, especially as the senior midwife was downstairs watching Match of the Day. Yes, despite my son Clive being born in hospital, Ruth insisted on having baby number two, Kate, at home. She was born in the very bedroom she used until she went to university. Nice really. Children should have a stable home.

We always knew we would have children and we were only married for three years when Clive was born. We decided that I would change my job and we would move house just a few months after his birth, but these so-called stressful situations do not seem to bother us. They are just little projects to be organised. His birth was quite good fun. Three days before he was due, Ruth, with a huge bump in front of her, was happily preparing to cook a chicken, as her parents were visiting the next day for lunch. Having attended pre-natal classes and being medically-minded, she suddenly realised that she was going into labour. Typically, she cooked the chicken, rang her parents with the news and packed a bag. Feeling a bit numb and apprehensive, I drove our Morris Minor to the new maternity wing in Gravesend Hospital. We laughed, nervously, when Ruth's waters broke in the lift, but we were also getting rather excited at the prospect. As the baby was obviously in a hurry, we bypassed the labour ward and entered the delivery area. We were temporarily abandoned and I had to run into the corridor calling for help, when the baby decided to arrive. The staff were so good, so professional. They gave me a mask, probably in case I frightened the baby, and four of them stood by for the imminent birth. First the head appeared and I stared him in the face in utter amazement. His little eyes were shut and I watched him closely as his mum kept pushing. Within a few moments his body popped out and shot across the waiting plastic sheet like a rocket. Fortunately, they caught him and wrapped him up warmly. 'What's his name?' they asked. 'We can't put Baby Brooks on his tag.' It was make-your-mind-up time, so I checked with Ruth and said, 'Clive'. Seeing your babies appear is a breathtaking experience.

Somebody told me that you should produce children bravely and knowingly and bring them up to the best of your ability. We have tried very hard to do that.

Just before Clive was born, I decided to change jobs, so I wrote to companies with large computer departments, offering my services as a business systems analyst. Applying directly cuts out the competition when replying to advertisements. Lucas Industries in the Medway towns happened to have a vacancy and wanted me, so I accepted and proceeded to find a house near to work. We had listed all the features we wanted in a new property, like detached with a spacious kitchen and big garden and we were sent details of one that ticked all the boxes. The price was very important, but an amazing thing happened. House prices were rising very rapidly in 1972 and our first home seemed to have gone up in value from £4,750 in 1968 to an estimated £7,000. The new house was on the market for £10,500, which was quite a big gap in those days. However, before going to see the prospective new home, we got an estate agent to visit us in Gravesend and give an up-to-date valuation on our present home. We were absolutely staggered, when he said £9,000. He put it on the market, whilst we drove to see the house in Medway. We took one look, loved it and left baby Clive with some kind new neighbours, Doris and John, while we completed the deal. We nipped down to the seller's estate agent and our building society that afternoon, remembering that we now had a baby and retrieved him from a doting Doris. Our first house sold for the asking price of £9,000 just three days after it was advertised and we moved into the new place within two months. We are still there and happier than ever.

Our very friendly neighbours quickly told us that our 'close' had its own sports and social club with several embryonic sections, like the football team, drama group, art club and the drinking parties. We got involved in everything and it has been a real treat. Thirty-seven years later, we still have the same people around us.

Ruth got good newspaper reviews for her acting, which was put on for the public. My efforts were purely private, for the children of the club. My finest moment was the first and only time that I have worn a bra. Believe me, chaps, it is not easy. My excuse is that I was playing Widow Twanky in panto. It was a devil to get my arms round my back to fasten the bra. Yes, ladies, Ruth did eventually tell me how to do it the easy way. You have to fasten it at the front of your body before bringing the cups round to the correct position and popping your arms in. That is unless you can get one of those nursing bras that fasten at the front. Enough of this.

Every summer we had a special day at the seaside with our neighbours, playing games with the children and enjoying a picnic. Clive was just able to walk when we first went to Minnis Bay on the north Kent coast. We were having some food on a large grassy area, which was separated from the beach by a minor road to the car park. You try to be good, attentive parents, but toddlers can be spontaneous and fast. Just as I looked down for Clive, a voice boomed 'Whose is this child?' It was a huge policeman, rotund like PC Plod in Enid Blyton's tales of Noddy. He was walking towards our group from the other side of the road. Under his arm was Clive in his bright red, easily recognisable coat. Ruth, to her own surprise as much as mine, instantly hid behind a bus shelter, while I stepped forward to receive Clive and be told off by this perfect policeman. I can picture him to this day and he was quite right in what he said about keeping a close eye on your children.

We organised a fabulous street party for the Queen's Silver Jubilee in 1977. There was a long table for food and drink, bunting everywhere and games all day. I have a super photograph of our two little ones holding onto the rope in a tug of war with the neighbours. I was really pleased that in 2002 we had the interest and energy to close the road again and celebrate Her Majesty's Golden Jubilee.

We have had so many happy times in our present home, but there have been one or two that were slightly alarming, like the fire. 'Wake up,' insisted Ruth. 'I can smell smoke and hear a crackling noise. We've got a fire.' We grabbed Clive and Kate, aged six and four, ran down the stairs through thickening smoke, saw a fire in the kitchen and put the kids on the wall in the front garden. They seemed unconcerned and just sat there. I ventured into the kitchen, found the waste bin alight and quickly, but carefully put it out with water. Meanwhile, Ruth was frantically dialling 000. She should have been dialling 999, but in the smoky conditions her finger found the end spot in the old-style rotating dial, so it became 000. I told her to forget it, as the fire was out, so we collected the kids and went back to bed. Neither the fire brigade nor the neighbours knew a thing about it. We had a party the previous evening and I suppose that somebody accidentally left a smouldering cigarette end in an ash tray, which was emptied into the bin. Anyway, there was fire damage to a cupboard, some clothes and wall tiles. I then had a very disappointing experience with the insurance company. I put in a carefully calculated claim of £105 for the ruined items, offering to tile the wall and redecorate myself, at no cost to them. They telephoned and told me they would pay £65. I was shocked and we started to argue and barter. I really needed the money to fix the damage, so I was quite angry, by my standards. I did ask whether they were a proper insurance company or barrow boys, as they slightly increased their offer a number of times. I eventually got £95.

Once again I was sleeping peacefully one night, when Ruth informed me that there was somebody on our extension roof. Why is it that it is always women that notice these things and men that investigate? I put on the light and opened the curtains, but saw no sign of an intruder. Then our doorbell rang. I scurried downstairs to see through the glazed front door two very large figures.

'Police. May we come in?' asked one of the men. 'We saw your light was on. Have you been out?'

'No, we haven't been out. We heard a noise. Could you pop your IDs through the letter box please?'

The IDs looked fine, so I opened the door to find two huge policemen and an equally large, black, panting dog. The animal was clearly very keen to catch villains.

'May we take him through your garage and into the back garden please? We are chasing some men.' They were very polite and I quickly let them through.

Ruth and I looked out of our rear bedroom window and every back garden was alight with police torches. We could see much activity and hear many raised voices. We then looked out of the front of the house and there were several policemen and six police vehicles, including two dog-handlers' vans. We went to bed and heard no further reports on what had happened. Again, none of our neighbours heard a thing.

I was quite handy about the house, making and repairing things. One morning I decided to take a chisel to an unsightly piece of wood glued to the bottom of a big, old sideboard. I was lying on the floor trying to hammer this rusty old tool against the wood, when the chisel slipped and glanced against my forehead, just above my eyes. It was a fairly small cut and not much blood, but Ruth insisted that I went to the hospital for vaccination against tetanus. It was quite well-known that certain bacteria getting into cuts could cause tetanus, commonly known as lockjaw, which leads to muscle contraction and can be fatal. When I was seen in the casualty department, I was first given an injection in the buttock, which wasn't very nice, then sent to another room to await a nurse. She did not explain what she was going to do, but asked me to lie down on a bed, while she fetched a sterile sheet, which was folded in four. She cut off one corner to make a central hole and, as she unfolded it, I saw this and quite unreasonably got the giggles. She looked pleasantly puzzled, so I asked whether she was going to place the cloth over my head with the wound exposed through the little hole for some reason. Yes, she was going to do that and insert just one black stitch to pull the cut together and help the skin heal nicely. I think the stitch was more to teach me a lesson about handling tools correctly, but my strange sense of humour had kicked in and I found it all rather amusing.

On 2 April 1982, Argentina invaded the Falkland Islands and so began the Falklands War. Clive was ten years old and this was the first significantly unpleasant incident in his young life. He was clearly aware of what was going on and told me of a lad at school whose dad went to fight. So, as a parent, one has to give children a view on war and we had a chat about the reasons for the conflict. Not easy, but parenthood is quite a challenge, if taken seriously. One of our neighbours, Terry, was a petty officer and had to go with his ship. We gave him a good send-off, but an even bigger welcome back with a full-blown street party. There was sheer joy on Terry's face as he entered the road and saw what we had laid on for him, especially the big banner bearing his name. The conflict lasted just over two months and 255 members of the British task force were killed, including a chap local to us. Three ladies at Port Stanley sadly died too.

We were the traditional taxi-driver parents, ferrying our kids to and from various sporting events, clubs, musical activities, parties and, eventually pubs and nightclubs. 'As you sow so shall you reap' would run through my mind. How we behave towards our children now will affect their behaviour and attitudes for the rest of their lives, so we have to take great care with their upbringing.

A priority had to be love and security. No problem there. Ruth and I had received that, so it was natural to pass it on with cuddles, bed-time stories and open shows of affection. In order to give them a firm base, we made a point of not moving house. As we had a lovely home and great neighbours, it was fairly easy to stay put, despite being offered jobs as far away as Ipswich, Birmingham and Brazil!

We added opportunity to love and security by letting them try any sports or hobbies they desired. Several things clicked with them, including swimming, which we could all actively share, once I had taken some lessons myself! There was a slightly scary incident one Saturday at our local swimming baths, the Black Lion in Gillingham. It had a diving pool with the correct standard of boards at each height, including the very high top board. Clive and Kate usually went off the lower boards, but on this occasion three of us watched as Kate, aged four, clambered up the tall ladder to the very top board. There were several teenage lads posing there, probably not intending to dive, as little Kate crawled round their legs and stood on the business end of the board. They and we stared at her in wonder and some horror as she leapt off like a frog. It seemed to take ages for her to plop into the water and even longer for her to rise to the surface, before smiling and calmly swimming to the side. She always did seem to be brave. My neighbour John was amazed when Kate was escorted up our road by his son Philip and our Clive, who explained that she had fallen into a whole patch of stinging nettles, but did not even cry!

The kids chose the activities they enjoyed the most and continued them for several years. Kate had her Brownies, dancing and gymnastics, but added the more difficult hobbies of trampolining and playing the trombone. Clive tried most sports and won trophies for football and table tennis. I was fascinated by what his lawn tennis coach taught him. It seems that I had always held the racket wrongly and hit the ball very wrongly. Once Clive picked up the correct technique, he looked very good. However, his greatest personal triumph was in the Medway Open Table Tennis tournament. This was a handicap event including the best adult players in Kent and beyond. Clive was fifteen years old and, like other young boys, was given some points start against the more experienced, high-ranking and adult players. I always watched his sports and often got myself over-excited, which is not too wise really. The knockout tournament started in the morning and was expected to finish around tea-time, but I was going to bring Clive home as soon as he was eliminated. We also had friends coming to dinner in the evening, but I did not really expect a problem with the timing of it all. Well, he won round after round. The organisation was not very efficient, so it was about 5pm when he reached the quarter final of the singles, where it would be very tough to progress any further. Two hours later, due to the ladies competition and doubles matches, he was still waiting to play, so I reluctantly left him in order to greet our friends. Clive had instructions to telephone me when he needed picking up. After a while, he rang to say he had played and won his game, so he was in the semi-final against a leading adult player. He had exceeded all expectations and I wished him good luck. Although I wanted to watch him, it went through my mind that he might be better off without me worrying, advising, shouting etc. Another telephone call and he had won his match and was about to play the final that minute. Exciting isn't it? I rushed to the venue in my car and found him in the telephone box, as arranged, clutching the winner's trophy. I wished I had seen him win, but supposing I had put him off?! Apparently, the final was so late that only about five people, including the finalists, were still in the building. I was very proud of him and nothing has changed to this day. I am proud of both my children. They have always tried their best.

I knew that we had created a happy environment for the children, so education was the other big issue. I suppose most parents would like to see their children achieve more than they had. We supplied plenty of books and read to them every night before they went to bed. We took a great interest in their school work and encouraged them with their homework. Without too much pressure, we managed to impart that same work ethic at school that Ruth and I had understood. We live in an area that still takes the Eleven Plus examination to determine whether or not you go to grammar school. Fortunately, they both passed and that initial 'hurdle' had been cleared. They worked hard, went to university and obtained good degrees. Clive went on to become a chartered accountant, which I had in mind for myself at that stage, but could not face further study. Kate works in finance at the same university where she obtained her degree, having first worked outside in industry. It gives me pleasure that they have fertile brains, good use of English and want their own children to have a great education too.

Finally, I had hoped that all this would bring the kids a quality much needed in the modern competitive world, which is confidence. I wish that I had been blessed with a more enterprising disposition at a younger age, but I think Clive and Kate have just about the right amount.

In order to broaden their horizons, as they say, we also took the children to many other countries, forty to be exact. We hoped that they would enjoy travel, but always return to the best country of all, England.

We had some fabulous holidays abroad with the kids, in addition to those I have described in the previous chapter. I suppose that the first one in 1982 was the most memorable, as it was for four weeks in the United States and Canada. We saw New York and four major cities in California, before visiting Toronto, Calgary and driving through the Rockies to Kamloops.

It took three years to recover from what we spent, but I regret not one fabulous moment. Well, maybe I slightly regret riding on a giant swing called Montezuma's Revenge! The kids and Ruth loved it. I shut my eyes until it was over. We spent a few days in each of Las Vegas, Los Angeles, San Francisco, and San Diego and accidentally drove over the Mexican border, where our hire car was not allowed to go. Fortunately they let us turn around and drive back into the States without a word being said. I suspect that it was a common mistake in those days. We walked into Mexico for a quick look, but it was rather hot and dusty so we scurried back over the border fairly quickly. Obviously, we visited Disneyland as well as Sea World, Knott's Berry Farm theme park and many other popular attractions in California. The kids loved the glitter of Las Vegas. We stayed in an inexpensive motel on the Strip, which Clive spotted because it had a raised swimming pool and you could see through portholes in the sides. Unusually, Ruth and I fell asleep on sun beds that evening and awoke very late to find the kids still swimming around the warm blue water chatting to some new American friends. I love the way that children simply ask one another their names and ages, then start playing together. On the second evening, we trusted them to watch the entertainment on their own in a children's part of the casino called Circus Circus. They had some money to gamble, as we also did in an adjacent, adult area. Ruth and I had changed just five dollars into quarters and were playing a machine for quite some time, until we were down to four coins. As we needed to check up on the kids, I put all four coins into the slot for quadruple odds, before pressing the button for the last time. We were walking away, looking over our shoulders at the machine, when we saw a winning line come up. We then heard that marvellous noise that attracts attention, as dozens of quarters tumbled out. We caught them in a large pot and wondered how much we had and whether we could convert them into dollar bills. The Americans, of course, had the answer. The cashier tipped our pot into a counting device that registered seventy-two dollars or about thirty-seven pounds! The kids were very impressed with that, but sad to be dragged off to bed.

Whilst in San Francisco, my son egged me on to drive down Lombard Street, 'the crookedest (most winding) street in the world', which was easier than it looked. We also visited the former prison on Alcatraz Island, where the guide kindly locked us in solitary confinement for a few minutes to help us appreciate what life was like for inmates. As our family seems to repeat things at each generation, we took my son's children to Alcatraz in 2006 and Clive drove down Lombard Street in 2009.

That trip to the USA was the first time we had seen large numbers of obese people, a problem that we now have in Britain. As we queued to enter a theme park on a very hot day, Clive, aged ten, removed his shirt to try to cool down. He was abruptly told that males could not come in bare-chested. It seemed ironic that we were standing behind huge folk in shorts with acres of unsightly flesh and our little lad was asked to cover up.

Oh, I must tell you how we paid off the credit card bill. It was huge, as was the potential interest if we only paid part of it. I explained to the kids, who had significant savings, that if they loaned their money to me, I would pay the credit card bill in full and give the interest I would have been charged to them, not the bank. I would also repay their lump sums fairly quickly, making sure that they ended up in profit. They went for it straight away in a kindly, matter of fact manner, which pleased me. Obviously, I stuck to the promise and their investments took off again. We always try to keep money within the family and give as little as possible to banks.

Both Clive and Kate had holidays abroad with their schools, usually skiing. It was good to give them that bit of freedom to travel with pals, as we had both been very fortunate to experience that whilst schoolchildren ourselves. Strangely, we did not seem to get the full stories of what happened on these trips until the children had grown up and felt able to tell us. Maybe they thought that we would ban future journeys, if we knew of the dangers. In Kate's case, she was on a school coach trip to Austria with her best friend, who was asthmatic. Apparently, halfway up a mountain, some side and rear wheels of the coach went over the edge of a sheer drop. The children were evacuated from the coach with my daughter helping her friend by gently easing her off the coach. They ascended the steep hill in blizzard conditions and Kate's friend became rather breathless and poorly, as her inhaler had been left on the coach. Fortunately, a teacher helped to keep the lass calm and her breathing returned to normal. According to Kate, another vehicle had to pull the coach to safety. It is just as well that you do not know these things at the time.

As a young adult, Clive casually mentioned a school skiing trip, where he accidentally left the slope on a sledge and crossed a main road between cars.

Over several consecutive summers, Clive and Kate, in their early teens, would sleep most summer nights in a tent pitched in our back garden. They had a sponge mattress, sleeping bags, lighting and a television powered by a car battery. Our garden is enclosed by dense trees and shrubs and, as it turned out, was quite safe. We left the back door unlocked all night so that they could come in and use the toilet. They thoroughly enjoyed camping on the lawn and we only worried a little.

In the winter, I often found myself at Clive's football matches tying football nets to posts with frozen fingers in order to get the game started. I expect many dads remember that task. It was worth it as Clive's primary school team, Parkwood, won the league and cup double. His Sunday team, Kingsferry Bredhurst, were very good too, so there was plenty of boys' football for me to watch and enjoy. The most exciting match was the schools cup final held under floodlights at the ground of Chatham Town FC. Parkwood wore Spurs' blue and white kit, whilst their opponents were in Liverpool's red strip, so that suited us fine. These teams of ten year olds gave everything and fought out an exciting draw with two goals each. The head of schools football said it was such a good game that he wanted the two sides to share the trophy and not seek a result by playing extra time. I think they were almost exhausted anyway. I know I was.

As teenagers, the kids would enjoy skiing at the local ski slope while Ruth and I watched them and supped a cup of coffee. We could see how much they enjoyed it, as they returned to the top of the steep white slope time and time again. In the winter, the four of us would also take plastic sacks to the hills for 'tobogganing' in the snow. We would return home bruised but exhilarated. These were good times.

I had pointed out to the kids the merits of supporting Tottenham Hotspur FC or Spurs and luckily they were convinced. I took Clive to his first game when he was six and we went to as many home games as possible, as well as some away matches, until he went to university. Our trips included two FA Cup Finals and a League Cup Final at Wembley with the huge pleasure of watching many great players.

Whilst looking out of our kitchen window one Saturday, I noticed something that would help define how I acted towards other people in certain circumstances, particularly if I was fortunate enough to have grandchildren one day. Our neighbours Dave and Jill had three sons and that day the grandparents were paying a visit. Grandad Bert was a retired barber and reminded me a bit of my own dad, except that Bert had a small, neat moustache. I was watching him in the front garden with the boys doing some bicycle maintenance and chatting away. I never really knew my own grandparents and Ruth and I had both lost our fathers by this time, but to the best of my knowledge grandads generally sat around drinking tea when they visited. Not Bert. He liked to make himself useful and interact with the boys at the same time. Now, why not? It takes the same amount of time to do something helpful as to do nothing at all. Just like Bert, I love helping my children and grandchildren, but more of them later.

Clive and I were often found kicking a ball around the local park, sometimes alone, but often with about eight other boys that I had crammed into the Ford Cortina. The local professional team was and still is Gillingham FC, who trained occasionally in that park. On one occasion, Clive chased a stray ball from me, which landed at the feet of a very young Steve Bruce, who kindly tapped it back. He was a strong young fullback and the Gills best player. He later found fame with Manchester United and went on to Premiership management, of course. Actually, as I write, he is just switching club managership from Wigan to Sunderland. Well, he is a Northumberland lad, so good for him, but I thought he supported Newcastle.

In the same park one day, I heard a lady anxiously calling to me from a distance. I saw that she had a large black and tan Alsatian dog, so I asked my son to stay where he was while I ran to see what she wanted. She had just sent her daughter to fetch her husband, as the dog had a ball lodged in its throat. The poor animal was very distressed and staggering around unable to breathe. She begged me to help save her pet, as it was her husband's ex-police dog and he would be devastated if it came to any harm.

I pulled open its mouth as wide as I could with both hands, imploring her to try to pull out the ball, but it was too small for a large dog and was firmly stuck at the back of its throat. I tried everything, including desperately slapping its back, but it got steadily weaker and stopped breathing as I held it up still clawing at the ball. It was clearly dead and I lowered it to the ground. In hindsight, I suppose I needed a pointed instrument like a screwdriver to somehow skewer the ball and prise it out, but I didn't have one. I left as the girl returned with her dad and simply saw him staring at the body. We did not speak and I returned to my son, still waiting with his football.

I knew from experience to be very careful what to throw for a dog. I described earlier what happened, when, as a boy, I threw a sharp stick for our poodle Freda and it pierced her upper palate.

Back to Spurs for a moment. When Kate started dating her boyfriend Alex at the University of Hertfordshire, they lived close to where Spurs Reserves played their home games, St Albans. Fortunately, Alex was a fan of our club too, but that was not the only reason that I took an immediate liking to him. Calling him a really nice lad does not seem to describe him highly enough, but that is how he came across. When Kate first brought him to our house, she left him in the lounge with Ruth and popped into the kitchen, where I was getting some drinks. We just looked at one another and she could tell how much I liked him.

We are now in 1995 and I was working in London. This meant that I could drive from the office in Holborn to their digs, pick up Kate and Alex and watch the Reserves every fortnight. When our daughter and now hubby moved to Stevenage, Spurs Reserves switched to that town's ground for their home games, so it was all rather convenient. One evening we were watching the Reserves warming up and saw the tallest and thinnest young footballer that I have ever seen. He looked surprising skilful. At that moment, our manager George Graham and his wife walked past us, so I asked George the name of this lad. He smiled and said, 'Peter, er Peter something. He's very good.' An old lady standing in front of us turned and said, 'It's Peter Crouch'. Leaping forward to April 2009, I watched Peter, by then a Portsmouth player, score an excellent goal for England against the Ukraine in a World Cup qualifying match. Leaping even further forward to August 2009, Peter has rejoined Spurs and scored again!

Kate married Alex in April 2003 and I had that enormous pleasure of spending some time talking alone with her just before 'giving her away'.

I thought that Kate was beautiful, both on the outside and inside. I still think so and love her very much.

One of our interests that has not yet rubbed off onto our children is our love of antiques. It started with the death of Ruth's great aunt Maude. She and her husband Harry married rather young in 1900 and rented the same terraced house in Tottenham, north London until Harry died in his eighties. They had no children, rarely spent any money and never used their best furniture, which was in the 'front room'. Harry was a legend in Ruth's family for not wanting to pay 'Income Tax'. His nephew, Syd, Ruth's dad, explained that it was compulsory. Also, it transpired that he spent his working life and retirement collecting money. He would convert his wages and pension into five pound notes, iron them flat and make them into piles of £100. These were all progressively bundled into mouse-proof Oxo tins and hidden in the loft or under the floorboards. Fortunately, following her husband's death, Maude divulged this to Syd before she moved out. I know that on one visit, my father-in-law found £12,000 hidden away, which was quite a bit forty years ago. Ruth and I were asked by her dad whether we would like some of the fine old furniture from their house. The items were stylish, but not exactly modern and would not go with our mixture of G Plan and melamine-topped tables. A decision had to be made. Should we stay as we were or go Victorian? A compromise would be disastrous. We opted for the latter and have had the great pleasure of adding more furniture, much glassware and many appropriate paintings to the first items of furniture we were fortunate to inherit.

Two of the pictures hanging in our dining room are of Ruth's great-great-grandparents, painted in the year 1870. Ruth's mother had a very sweet cousin named Rosie, who was a truly Victorian spinster. She had been a clerk with the East India Company, which started trading commercially and ended up ruling large parts of India. Rosie was eccentric, which was probably why she liked me. I would pop in to see her when travelling near her north London home on business. Her sitting room was very cluttered and, although she had many chairs, most already had something resting on them. She would find me a space to sit down and make me a cup of tea. Rosie always used a cup and saucer, of course. She wanted to give me and Ruth her old, family items, like the paintings, as well as letters that her grandparents exchanged before they died. They were beautifully written and very touching. Rosie passed away in her eighties, having spent her declining years living on cream cakes and brandy. She kindly left Ruth

£1500, with which she bought herself a little black Mini, as we only had my company car at the time and she deserved some increased mobility.

I digressed from the kids, but I realise that we often come to certain hobbies and interests later in life, like gardening, family history and antiques. I cannot see our two putting Victorian furniture in their modern homes, but they certainly like a pleasant, well-kept garden. I mostly want them to be part of the modern world and be able to do their own thing, as they say.

As a footnote to trying our best for the children, I would mention an incident at one of our recent Christmas Eve parties. We have had an open house for friends on that day every year since 1981. It started when my colleagues and I found the pubs were closed at twelve noon and we could not celebrate the start of the holiday. As we lived near my work, I invited everyone back to our house for a drink. Ruth was surprised, but was very game and the kids loved it. Over the years, the numbers attending our party peaked at 104, which was rather crowded that year. Nowadays, we attract about fifty pals and I thank them all for their continued friendship. Many tell us that their Christmas always starts at our party and we must never stop, so we won't. At our 2006 party, a friend of mine had been chatting to my son, and then came to tell me what Clive had said. He had told our guest that his childhood had been 'idyllic'. I often think about that with pleasure among the many enduring moments of joy that my children have brought me. We love them and they love us, which makes me incredibly happy.

-10-

SPORTY AT LAST

'If you can fill the unforgiving minute
With sixty seconds' worth of distance run'
(If by Rudyard Kipling, 1910)

My two sisters were our family's award winning athletes at school. I believe that Mum and Dad had been pretty good too, whilst at school in Bethnal Green. However, my brother and I, though fit and lively enough, did not excel at games. Dad enjoyed watching most sport, in particular athletics, football and boxing. In 1954, when I was seven, we watched Chris Chataway, who was still running in 2009, beat Vladimir Kuts in the 5000 metres at the old White City. It was 'live' on television. I used to run around the house and stop at Dad's chair, then he would say 'Chataway went thataway' and off I would dash. That was the same year that Roger Bannister became the first man to run a mile in less than four minutes. Growing up in east London, Dad was well aware of lads using boxing to escape the poverty trap and he saw many a great fight at the famous York Hall in Bethnal Green. Though not a particular fan of boxing, I did sit with Dad in 1963 and watch 'our Enry' (Henry Cooper) knock down Cassius Clay in round four. Although delighted by that great punch, my Dad said he thought Clay would really lay into Cooper in round five, which he duly did. This caused our man to bow out with a badly-cut eye. Clay later became known as Mohammed Ali and the rest is history.

As a little lad, I asked Dad which he liked best out of football, boxing and athletics, hoping he would say football. I was disappointed when he said boxing, then athletics, then football. When I asked why not football, he said that the better team did not always win. He said it was more likely and more deserved in boxing and running, where a man was on his own, unaided by team-mates or specialist equipment, as in some sports. He still loved Spurs and never seemed to mind that I was not sporting, but very pleased that I was academic. However, he lived long enough to find that as an adult, I was dabbling in football, jogging and squash.

Energetic, but not very good at football, I actually joined a Sunday football team, when I was twenty-four. We moved to our present home and our neighbours had a team, all of whom, except me, were keen footballers at school. In a short career at fullback, I achieved my ambition of playing adult soccer and understanding it from a player's point of view rather than simply as a spectator. This included the banter and the dreadful, basic, Sunday League dressing rooms. My most memorable match was a goalless draw against an army team. A strong, super-fit squad came at us for ninety minutes and I gained immense satisfaction in helping to keep them at bay.

I was equally mediocre at squash, to which, like many sports, I introduced my son. He was able to beat me at all of them whilst still a young boy. I was that bad and he was that good. I did not even try my daughter's main sport – trampolining! I seem to know how things should be done, but do not always have the ability to do them well myself. I showed a friend, who had no talent for racket sports, how to play squash and he quickly won our company championship against some very good players. Perhaps I was becoming a teacher or coach.

Then it happened. I knew I was capable of jogging a couple of miles, when I got into a life-changing conversation with a neighbour at a late night party. This was in 1982, when I was thirty-five. John was twelve years my senior and told me that he was training to run his first marathon. Now, this feat was uncommon at the time, but the London Marathon was two years old and there was a growing keenness for running long distances in Britain, as well as various other countries like the USA. When I said I would love to run a marathon, John suggested that I have a run with him the next morning, if I wished. The challenge was that it was 4am when we discussed this, having drunk far too much, and his training run started at 6am!

After less than two hours sleep, I was at his door in my vest, shorts and trainers. John, a professor at City University in London, explained that he ran his long distances at this time on a Sunday, so that his hobby would not interrupt his family life. This was another lesson I stored away from somebody that I respected. He also explained that he was running ten miles that morning in two circuits of five miles, at eight minutes per mile. We agreed that I would try to do the first five miles and trot to my house. After about four miles, he praised my ability to keep up a good pace, which was pleasing, but I realised that I would indeed have to quit when we passed near to home on the first lap. I thanked him and ran to my house.

As I stopped in my porch and opened the front door, I realised that something dramatic was happening to my body. I was only just able to mount the stairs, as my legs stiffened horribly. In a bit of a daze, I managed to undress and stand in the shower. On slipping into bed, around 6.50 am, I melted into a deep sleep till late that morning. I was unable to walk without great pain for several days, but had got the bug!

I trained hard and soon ran a tough, hilly half marathon in Canterbury at just under seven minutes per mile. That race ended inside the St Lawrence Cricket Ground and I managed a sprint finish, overtaking many runners just inside the gate. Unfortunately, it was not the finish, as we still had to run round the entire pitch before reaching the line. I was shattered, but refused to let anyone catch me, as I coughed and spluttered my way to the end. I felt a little embarrassed as I staggered as briskly as possible over the line, almost vomiting. With this experience behind me, I decided to enter the 1983 London Marathon. The application procedure was not as simple as it is now. Having acquired and completed the entry form, you had to hand it in at one of a hundred post offices around Britain at a certain time on a specific date. Each office would accept one hundred entries, on a first come first served basis, making a total field of ten thousand runners. Another consideration was that each person in the queue could hand in up to four forms, so you needed to be no more than twenty-fifth in the queue to be sure of a successful outcome. Well, my nearest post office on the list was in Chatham, so, on the previous day Ruth and I went to see exactly where I would need to line up the following morning. Shock, horror, there were already ten people in the queue! I had no chance of gaining a place in the race unless I acted immediately. Another anxious-looking chap was joining the line and instructing his wife to bring him supplies, so I interjected. I suggested that he queued for both of us, but I return later with a sleeping bag and do the night shift. We agreed that as he was eleventh in the queue, there could be no more than forty applications ahead of us. Also, as a sign of good faith I gave him my entry form, which was in my wallet for some reason. When I got back in the early evening, his wife had brought his form, which he handed to me, and we parted with a handshake. The line of potential runners was massive, but nobody minded when I swapped places with my new friend and set up my camp bed. It was odd sleeping on the pavement, but a public toilet had been deliberately left open and some jovial policemen patrolled and checked that we were okay. Although it was winter, I was very snug in a balaclava helmet and anorak, all tucked up inside a sleeping bag. Fortunately, it did not rain that night. I woke long before 9am, when the post office opened to receive entries. My new pal turned up to join me in handing over our forms for what was to prove to be a successful application. We shook hands again and departed. I didn't know his name, but I hope he did well.

The race itself was a most exciting occasion and thanks to the willingness of helpers and sponsors, I raised my first donation to charity with around seven thousand pounds for the British Heart Foundation. I also managed to overtake and beat Jimmy Savile in his gold lame suit! At fifty-six, he was twenty years older than me, but he certainly knew how to execute a marathon. Although I ran a practice marathon before attempting that first public run, I went off too fast in the London and 'hit the wall', but literally. Crudely, hitting the wall is when you run out of sugar energy and try to burn fat. For a short while, you can become dizzy and weak. When this happened to me, I wasn't expecting it, but I aimed for a public loo and stumbled into the wall, banging my head. After a few bewildering moments, I made myself start running again. It was some time after that when I caught up with Jimmy. It taught me not to get carried away and begin too fast, which is a common problem for novices. Since then, I have had the pain and pleasure to run the London another eight times, as well as our local Gillingham in Kent, the New York, Boston, Paris and Edinburgh. I never hit the wall again, but was dogged for a few years by sciatica. On three occasions, a physiotherapist had to work on my leg to relieve the pain, even the day before a race. I hate not being able to do something that my mind was fixed on achieving. Having apparently got over sciatica one year, I ran the London with my friend Dave, who was strong and athletic, but this was his first twenty-six miler. My sciatica returned after only six miles, so there was just the twenty to go, dragging one leg and wincing. We kept chatting until we crossed the line, hand-in-hand, in under four hours. Dave said it was probably his physical strength and my mental strength that got us both round. I have to agree and was pleased with the time, all things considered.

Another race I took part in was Sir Bob Geldof's 'Run the World', which was six miles. The venue was Folkestone, to where all my family had moved. When I first decided to run long distances, I bought a great little book on how to run a marathon by British athlete Bruce Tulloh and followed it religiously. This included not eating within four hours of the start of a run. However, only two hours before this particular race, I popped in to see Mum. I was both stupid and weak-willed when I allowed her to give me lunch, followed by pudding. I did not want it, but found I was unable to say no to her nor to explain why it mattered. It always pleased her to see her little boy tuck in to his dinner. My Mum and sisters had never seen me run and turned out to support me, along with Ruth as usual. I think my sporty sisters were even more surprised than I was when I got home in forty-one minutes, rather near the front of the race. It seemed incongruous that I could feel comfortable and do a fairly good time with all that food inside me. It is a pity that Dad didn't live to see me do anything sporty, not that he loved me less for it.

In May 1991, they completed the last section of the M20 motorway and put on a day of fun along that stretch, just before declaring it open to traffic. People cycled, rode horses, scattered wild flower seeds along the verges, abseiled from the bridges or just strolled and enjoyed the brilliant sunshine. I entered the M20 Missing Link Half Marathon, which is a little over thirteen miles up and down the motorway lanes, while Ruth scattered seeds. Despite the intense heat, I felt good and was really determined, coming home in seventeenth place.

There was a little incident on the plane to New York to run their marathon that put us in our place. Ruth had secretly organised the trip for my fiftieth birthday in 1997. She proudly told the lady next to her that I was fifty and was going to run the marathon. The lady replied that she had given her husband the same trip for his seventieth birthday. I hope he did well.

There have been some really nice races, like the Great North Run (thirteen miles) when the ex-Newcastle and England footballer Peter Beardsley started the race and slapped all our hands as we passed by. The race starts in Newcastle and ends in South Shields and I can recommend it.

I would regularly run local half-marathons to keep fit and raise money. The route of the race around Gillingham in Kent is very hilly and, fortunately, I am good on hills, as that's where I train. Clive once cycled the route with me, but remembers being unable to keep up with me on the uphill sections. It was even better when I overtook groups of very good runners from clubs like Blackheath Harriers as they chugged onwards and upwards. It was the first time I had heard bad language in a race!

In the year 2001, Ruth and our daughter-in-law Victoria entered the London Moonwalk, a 26-mile all-night trek around the capital raising money to fight breast cancer. The event was chiefly for women, but a few men also took part, like me. Well, having trained the girls, I was not going to miss out on spending eight or nine hours with thousands of ladies wearing pink bras, was I?

It was good to take part in a few races with Clive, when in his early thirties. We did a half marathon and several 10ks. Once he learned not to go off too fast and how to time his race properly, he did, of course, beat me. Good.

A few years ago, I met up with my best friend Alan from grammar school days and he was clearly surprised that I was a runner. He had been a good all-round sportsman and remembered, politely, that I was not!

Lastly on racing incidents, I did fail to take part in one run. It was the Great South Run in Portsmouth on a Sunday in 2007. It was only ten miles, but I trained hard. Ruth and I spent a satisfying Saturday sightseeing, followed by a delicious seafood evening meal. In hindsight, this was a big mistake. I was dreadfully ill in the night with non-stop diarrhoea. The race was due to start at 10am and it was a twenty minute drive to get there from our hotel. By 6am, Ruth was driving around looking for an all-night chemist or doctor. She found a surgery open and luckily it was only five minutes from the hotel, as I dared not leave the vicinity of a loo. The doctor was great and he realised that despite my weak condition I still wanted to run. He prescribed various things which Ruth obtained for me and I took them. Unfortunately, by 10am the medicine had not had time to take effect. In other words I still could not trust my bowels in a car for twenty minutes nor the inconvenience and embarrassment of diarrhoea at the start or during a race! I had to give up and two years later I am still a little annoyed. Another hour and I could have got round that ten miles and maybe done a decent time. It was difficult to go home without having run and I had something of an empty feeling in my stomach, as well as my bowels.

Most of my old friends start our conversations with 'Are you still running?' I feel obliged to explain that I will run for as long as I am able, then I will walk, and then crawl. Believe it or not, I try not to lecture anybody, but here is why I still run:

1. I want to be physically and mentally healthy for myself and my family
2. Running is the easiest way to exercise your heart and keep fit
3. It is inexpensive and easy to learn
4. It is readily available to everyone, regardless of age or location
5. You can run alone, with a partner or in a group
6. I can think and plan whilst running, which is relaxing and relieves stress (I've had pressure, but I don't allow stress to take hold)
7. Running improves self-esteem and confidence and makes you feel good
8. Marathon running is the only time I will ever be in the same competition as the best in the world!

I run alone, but I am never lonely.

-11-

THERE'S NO WAY WE'RE HAVING THE ******* INTERNET (Expletive deleted)

'If at first you don't succeed, call it version 1.0'
(Anon)

I had made good progress in my career with Lucas and in 1979 I was given responsibility for the introduction of computerised business systems across England and several overseas branches. I met some great people, especially two senior colleagues Mike and Bob, who taught me a lot about myself, as well as how to do the job professionally. The early computer systems were financial, like payroll and the ledgers, but I also saw the introduction of word-processing, spreadsheets, e-mail and shop floor production systems. In those days it was a ground-breaking and expensive event when I brought in computer-aided design technology to replace drawing boards in the engineering offices. We also began the introduction of stand-alone personal computers or PCs, which we could network together without the use of a mainframe computer. They were heady days that seem archaic now. We worked hard and conscientiously, but had a lot of fun too.

At least five of us in the Computer Department were married to a girl named Ruth. Not the same one, of course. Remarkably at one point, four Ruths were pregnant, including my one. What do you make of that? Anyway, we ran a book on which baby would arrive first, its sex and weight. As it happened, there were three girls, including our Kate, and one boy. We always had bets on a new baby's details. If nobody was absolutely correct, the baby got all the prize money.

One Ruth is still a good friend after nearly forty years and we have spent many a happy evening playing cards and eating Chinese food with her and her late husband Rod, together with Ian and Doreen from that same era. I have no problem mixing business with pleasure and some colleagues have become really good pals.

Strange things happen, when you work in an office. It was ten minutes to twelve o'clock on a Tuesday lunchtime, when the normally quiet chap sitting at the next desk to me yelled, jumped from his chair and rushed from the office. John (yes, yet another John) returned half an hour later, looking rather flustered, and sat down, but I had meetings all afternoon and no chance to ask him what had happened.

The next day I felt compelled to ask what had occurred on Tuesday. He seemed quite embarrassed, but explained that he had suddenly realised that it was his wife Estelle's birthday that day and he was in big trouble. Now, Tuesday was early closing day in our area and all shops shut at twelve noon, so I felt even more compelled to ask what he had bought for his wife. It was a ghastly story.

'I drove top speed to the precinct and all the shops were shutting. I burst into Woolworth as they were trying to close the door and grabbed the first thing I saw.'

'Chocolates?' I enquired.

'Er, no,' he replied.

'Well what? A book, flowers, a plant? What?'

Sheepishly, he mumbled, 'An Airfix kit.'

'What!' I exclaimed. 'What sort of kit was it? What does it make?'

'A battleship.'

'You cannot be serious. What did she say?'

'She just cried.'

'Happy or sad?'

'Sad.'

A few months later, John and Estelle threw a party with the theme 'horrors and hookers'. If you are unfamiliar with this, then the man is most likely to come dressed as something horrible and the woman as a prostitute. You always get one couple where she comes as the horror and he dresses as either a lady of the night or a rugby player. We like a good fancy dress party and always make an effort to concoct realistic costumes. Ruth found it quite easy with a mini-skirt and plunging neckline, but I probably went a bit over the top. I had an ugly facemask, a long ginger wig and a humped back covered in a vile old brown blanket. The hosts' front door was opened by a female guest, dressed as a hooker. She took one look at me, screamed and ran into the kitchen, genuinely scared. Well, apart from me, the greatest effort made by any man was a pair of plastic Dracula teeth, so I stuck out like a sore thumb!

When things calmed down a bit and I removed the hump and mask, there was some slow dancing in the lounge. I manoeuvred until I found myself with Estelle. I just could not let that story of the birthday present rest, I'm afraid. 'What happened to the Airfix battleship?' I enquired. 'Oh, I've nearly finished it,' she smiled. 'Just some painting to complete plus the stickers to apply.' For once I was lost for words.

A most memorable fancy dress party had the very popular television programme Allo Allo as its theme. Ruth and I were giving some friends a lift to the venue, when an oncoming motorist flashed us to stop, so that he could seek our advice. Whilst speaking to us, he showed no reaction to the fact that I was dressed as a nun with a large black moustache and two of my friends were in full, authentic German officers' uniforms!

On one occasion, two good friends that I worked with at Lucas were preparing to build a wall in one of their gardens, when the pickaxe handle broke. They are two rather burly chaps and were dressed in their labouring clothes, when they set off to buy a replacement handle. As they needed some cash, they walked into a bank carrying the old pickaxe handle. Imagine the faces of the customers and staff when these two appeared, but fortunately they withdrew the money in the conventional way.

During my sixteen years with Lucas, there were many strange and memorable moments. Among the silly ones were the national shortages. First we had rumours that the country was running out of petrol, so everyone stocked up and caused a real shortage. Then it was sugar and the same thing happened. The silliest was the loo paper suddenly disappearing from the shops. Seriously, this initially led to the Personnel Department (now HR) appointing loo paper monitors. They stood in the entrance to each toilet area and actually asked you how many sheets you required, before carefully dispensing them. When all the paper ran out, we took computer printout to the cubicles. I absolutely drew the line at using the carbon paper in the multi-part sets. I wish I was kidding you about this, but I am not.

I always took a packed lunch to work. I found this to be cheaper, more convenient, more nourishing and quicker to eat, whilst working. I never really took a lunch break, as I found that a change was as good as a rest and there was always plenty to do. Once or twice, probably around Christmas time, I was lured into the restaurant. It had taken many years for certain old-style British companies to get rid of the ridiculous nonsense of four or more levels of restaurant, according to status, and to bring in a single dining facility open to all. Incidentally, I was once awarded a key to the senior management toilet. Anyway, the meals in our 'canteen' included dodgy sounding dishes like 'brown meat' and the disgusting 'spam fritters'. We did not know what the brown meat was, but the fritter was spam cooked in the greasiest batter imaginable. I once stabbed a fritter with a fork and a geyser of oily liquid shot above my plate. I am not fussy, but it was revolting and 'hard to swallow'. Unusually for me, I felt sick. On another occasion, whilst collecting a meal and approaching some round, insipid, white potatoes, my colleague asked for 'The boiled please.' The reply was, 'They're the roast, love.'

The worst culinary incident involved the tea trolley. This was wheeled round the offices by two tea ladies dressed in white overalls and hats. Initially, refreshments were free, but then there was concern that it was a taxable perk, so we were charged two old pence per cup. True, I assure you. Eventually, due to the cost of providing tea ladies, they were replaced by vending machines. These cost a hell of a lot more and the quality at that time was very poor, especially the powdered tea. However, we received reports that the now redundant tea urn had been cleaned out. It was a bit worrying that this event warranted attention, implying it was quite a rare occurrence. What was found trapped in the bottom of the urn explained the rather strange taste and khaki colouring of the tea we used to drink regularly. A rotten tea towel had obviously been disintegrating in the base of the urn for a very long time. I can still taste that tea after nearly forty years.

Another John, a friend and colleague of mine, had been blind from birth and was a very good computer programmer. He was a great guy and the first person I knew to take an Open University degree. He asked me to read all the material to him, so that he could convert it to Braille as I spoke. Fortunately, it was a maths degree, so I understood every word, symbol and formula. It took a long time and I got to know John quite well. I found him very brave and highly amusing. He was married to a lady with almost no sight, but an awareness of light and dark spaces. They had a bubbly little baby girl, who was sighted, and a lifestyle that I found both fascinating and fun. John was as independent as possible, so when his toilet bowl broke, he simply walked to a hardware shop and bought a new one.

'How did you get it home?' I asked.

'I took it out of the box and put it on my head, so that my hands were free for the white stick and shopping bag' he replied.

John could not see anyway, so walking through the street like that made no difference as far as he was concerned. Although he asked neighbours to read his mail to him, he would do nearly everything else himself, like mowing the lawn.

'How do you make sure that you have mowed straight and it looks neat?' I asked. Silly me.

'I don't. It doesn't really matter. I do my best. Sometimes I mow it in the dark. It makes no difference to us.'

I think John is a fantastic chap. I would sometimes walk to work with him, but he actually walked faster than me, so I had to deliberately quicken my pace. He would always take a short cut through the woods, even in the dark and in the winter! As he said, it made no difference to him. If it was wet or muddy, he simply wore boots.

Around that time, I was given responsibility for graduate recruitment, which involved organising the university 'milk rounds'. This was where we spoke to prospective employees, and then arranged second interviews for the most promising candidates. Many big companies did this to inject some graduates into the mix of staff coming through. My specific interest was in getting youngsters to train as computer programmers and systems analysts, depending on aptitude. We enjoyed great success with this, although it became hard to hang onto good staff in a competitive market. Generally, I was pleased to have such good quality people coming through the system. Apart from being academic, we made sure that they had common sense, were well-rounded and good communicators, so I was very surprised and slightly irritated when I read the remarks made on a student's forms by one of our company personnel managers. It read, 'I have seen this candidate and recommend that he receives a second interview. He is very bright, but has no idea about business and has poor communication skills, so I suggest that our IT department might be interested.'

I also remember being somewhat surprised by a minor incident when one of our newly appointed graduates popped into my office. One of my staff was renovating a village pond and I had promised to bring in some tadpoles from my own pond. I had a jar on my desk, when the new lad came in.

‘What’s that?’ he asked.

‘Do you mean the tadpoles?’ I responded.

‘Yes, those things in the jar. Do they become something?’

‘Well, these will be frogs’ I said. ‘Are you pulling my leg or do you really not know?’

‘No, but I think I have heard of them.’

Now, I don’t know about you, but I was really surprised and wondered how a sensible, clever twenty-two year old Englishman could miss or forget something pretty basic like the life cycle of the frog.

Speaking of universities and graduates, the manager in overall charge of the factory to which our office was attached was a sixty-year old engineer named Bill, who had worked his way up from the shop floor. A good bloke, but he had a bit of a problem with graduates coming straight into the business on a high grade and good salary. He also did not appreciate that we were not all called by the good old names of Tom, Jim, Fred, George and Harry. He called me ‘Lenny’ a few times before I realised that he was speaking to me and corrected him. ‘Larry’ was not really on his radar. Two really good young project managers of mine, Stuart and Rod, were known, innocently, as ‘Steve’ and ‘Ron’ and so it went on. If he thought that we had new-fangled names, then he would really struggle with what we hear nowadays. Bill often used that expression, ‘University? I went to the university of life.’ This began to grate on a very down-to-earth senior colleague of mine, who also had a degree. The next time Bill used that phrase on him, his reply was excellent. He said, ‘Look Bill, I went to both.’

Stuart and Rod were two young engineers who answered an advertisement to join our company and train as IT business systems analysts and I am so pleased that they did. Their early days with me were unusual insomuch as Rod accidentally gave me the wrong address of his home and did not get the job offer until I rang him to ask whether he was still interested! When Stuart joined me, I put him and his wife in a hotel until they could find a property to buy. His wife Ginny was so unhappy stuck there that Ruth and I invited them to dinner and actually had them living with us and the kids for many weeks. They seemed to enjoy it and became firm friends with the four of us. Rod and Stuart have had long, successful careers.

As computer technology changed, I enjoyed many business trips in the UK and abroad, investigating the new possibilities for business systems development. One trip in 1986 found me in New York with two colleagues. I had time to quickly show them the sights, as I had been before with Ruth. I took them up the tallest buildings, of course, without realising for quite some time that both suffered from vertigo and were scared stiff. Fortunately, they also wanted to overcome their fear and enjoy the opportunity. The tour included the magnificent Twin Towers of the World Trade Centre. What a dreadful day it was on September 11, 2001, when the whole complex in Manhattan was destroyed by two hijacked planes and so many innocent people died. Ruth and I returned in 2003 and paid our respects at 'Ground Zero'. A very moving place indeed.

After more than sixteen years with Lucas, I moved to my third job in 1988 with Lloyd's of London. It is not really a company, but a very interesting and wide-ranging insurance market. Again, I managed IT business processes, but I was now moving firmly into office systems with PCs, local area networks and email. I was also asked to train groups of staff, not in IT but in teamwork and various aspects of personal development. I used my own camera to video some of the outdoor activities, like getting across a stream by walking on one rope whilst holding on to another. Incidentally, ten years later, I found the video and sent a rather amusing, but anonymous section to the television programme You've Been Framed and they paid me £250! Very handy. Interestingly, these training courses included the most senior managers in the business and I guided them through a number of telling exercises. This was the start of something good, getting away from computers and towards people.

However, my next career move to London Electricity in 1991 was a temporary step back to computers with a position as office systems development manager. I suppose that I look for coincidences as well as things that go in cycles, but there are plenty of these phenomena about. In the year that I was born, 1947, the government published the Electricity Bill (legislation, not an invoice) and bought 190 companies, thus nationalising electricity. Less than a year before I joined London Electricity, the government sold twelve regional electricity companies and privatised it again.

I was amazed to find that all the directors and the majority of senior management at my new company did not want to see PCs spread across the business, but were happy with 'dumb terminals' linked to the mainframe. Spreadsheets were not in common use either, although the finance department were getting interested. I did some research and quickly promoted powerful, networked personal computers with the best modern packages, despite some opposition. I had proposals for email turned down several times, even by my boss who could not see any significant use for it. Unfortunately, it came to the company in an unregulated way due to a groundswell of opinion that we should have it. I was not able to define to the masses how it should be used to the best advantage for the company, so it ran amok. As for the Internet, it was very early days, but my team and I could see that any progressive or prestigious business in London ought to have a web site.

My first proposal for the Internet to my most senior director brought the response, 'There's no way we're having the f****** Internet here!' I never bothered to speak to him again and registered a domain name for our company. I had support from our corporate communications manager and one way or another we got Internet access rolled out in a controlled manner, despite it being described by many as pointless. Years later, I still think it is fantastic and my wife even accesses it via her telephone! I already had some detailed technical knowledge of computing using 'relational databases' on a mainframe or PC, so I knew exactly how data was accessed in that form of technology. However, I could barely fathom how the new search engines like Google worked so fast, considering that the vast variety of information was being held many miles away.

I have seen many other great technical innovations in the last twenty years. Apart from asking London Electricity for a company car, because I was used to having one, I also requested and got a mobile phone. In 1991, these were the size of a house-brick, but I thought it would be useful for contacting Ruth and the office whilst I was travelling. Hardly anybody had a mobile and I did not want to appear to be pretentious or to look like a 'yuppie'. I found it slightly embarrassing, but I managed to keep it fairly well hidden for a thing that size. I felt much better when I saw building site workers using them to communicate with colleagues several floors above them. These telephones soon spread like wildfire and I am never without one. Nowadays I text family and friends several times a day and love it! Keeping in touch is wonderful.

I wished that I had a mobile when Ruth and I were in London with the kids a few years earlier in 1988. We separated briefly, me with Clive whilst Ruth accompanied Kate. We had agreed to meet at one o'clock outside the Virgin store in Oxford Street. Well, Clive and I waited for a long time to no avail. As Clive was old enough, I left him outside the store whilst I found a telephone to ring Ruth's mother. This was an arrangement whereby Ruth and I could both phone Ethel to tell her where we were, if we got separated. I told Ethel not to worry, when she said she had not heard from Ruth. After another long wait outside Virgin, Clive and I walked to the nearest police station and hospital, where helpful people rang around for us, but there was still no sign of the girls. After telephoning Ethel again, Clive and I got the train home, where we were surprised, but relieved, to find Ruth and Kate. Having forgotten about the arrangement with her mum, Ruth had stood outside Virgin for an hour or so, then simply brought Kate home. It turned out that, unknown to us, Virgin had two stores in Oxford Street!

By the way, two pieces of modern technology that I really appreciated at home were the automatic washing machine and the power shower. Don't laugh, but the washing machine saved households many hours of tiresome work every week compared with the alternatives. Also, having washed my body in sinks, metal tubs and traditional baths for many years, I found the power shower really wonderful too, especially as I run nearly every day and a quick top-down wash is ideal. While I am feeling pleased with electrical aids, I must praise two other items that have helped me a great deal in saving work and producing good results. They are my splendid hedge trimmer and electric screwdriver. Two of my best buys.

On the subject of advances in technology, way back in 1974 I had my own secretary, who used a typewriter. 'Word-processing' was a recent invention and not widely available. Some folk still use typewriters in the present day, but compared to typing into a computer, as I am now, the functionality and convenience are worlds apart. A typist would sometimes have to re-type whole pages, if they could not correct a mistake by applying a white substance to the error and typing over it. Occasionally, I was tempted not to point out mistakes and ask for corrections, but I remember two particular errors that simply had to be changed. Something I said was 'passed by hand' had become 'passed by gland', so that had to go. Probably the worst typing error was at the end of a very important report, where I summarised how I was going to 'tackle the problems'. This appeared in the first draft as 'treble the problems'. It turned me into a very careful proof-reader!

In my adult lifetime, listening to music has leapt from gramophones to tape cassette players to iPods and beyond. What an incredible advance. Add to that the video recorder and Sky+, together with remote control. All we need now are better quality television programmes. I did not think I wanted a satellite navigation system in my car, but my son bought one for me anyway and it is terrific. It has got us in and out of towns and villages all over Europe with great success, saving us much time and grief!

A strangely prolonged journey was the reduction of smoking cigarettes at work and in public places. In the early 1990's, the company I worked for introduced a partial ban on smoking in the workplace. It was not allowed in most work areas, but was still permitted in managers' offices. After much fuss and nonsense, this ban was extended to the whole multi-story building, except the 'smoking room'. This hell hole was placed next to the restaurant, so that diners could have a fag after lunch. Lovely. We all experienced the thick clouds of smoke billowing out of the room. Being joined in the lift by someone that had just left that room was pretty ghastly too. I had grown up in a house where Dad smoked and it had never bothered me, even when I started work. Now that I was becoming used to cleaner air, it was getting quite awful to be exposed to the fumes and smell. It was some years before the smoking room was dismantled, as many employees still 'needed' to spend fifteen minutes of each working hour in that place. Then began the now familiar sight of smokers having a 'drag' outside on the pavement.

It was quite amusing when our company was bought by the French. Whilst I was giving a presentation, the new, continental board members started removing the apples, pears and bananas from the fruit bowl in order to use it as an ash tray, while they had a glass of wine.

'Sorry', said one of the English directors brave enough to speak up. 'We have a smoking ban in this building.'

'What do people do?' enquired one of our French friends.

'Smoke outside in the street, I'm afraid.'

'Then we will smoke outside in the street too,' he pleasantly replied.

'By the way, there's a ban on alcohol in the building too.'

That was a bridge or pont too far. Whilst fulfilling my IT systems management duties, I personally discovered bottles of good quality French wine stashed in directors and managers' rooms. Fortunately, I also shared the odd glass or three with some very interesting new colleagues. After all, an occasional glass of red wine is supposed to be good for you.

Over the years, I had got used to our trains being dirty and smelly. Fortunately, the smoking ban hit them too and I was amazed at the difference. Carriage upholstery had previously been ingrained with stale cigarette smoke, especially when damp from contact with raincoats. After the ban, the smell lingered for a while, but the change became much more obvious when new rolling stock was introduced. You may not be a fan of our train service, but believe me, that was a big improvement.

However, I usually drove into London and, for a while, took my son to his job in the City. Our route was via the busy Blackwall Tunnel. As we approached the tunnel one day, he noticed these great pieces of spiky scaffolding appearing above and beyond it. This turned out to be the start of the Millennium Dome and we watched it develop. We were surprised to find that these twelve spikes were permanent parts of the structure. Sadly, considering the enormous cost of the construction, I found the exhibition it contained to be most disappointing. The only bright spot was a celebration of Tommy Cooper, who we once saw in a live show. He was a comic genius and I laugh every time I think of him.

The expression 'rush hour', when you cannot rush, has frequently featured in my working life. The morning jams in Kent and London have sometimes been alleviated by the opening of new roads, but only temporarily, as the volume of cars has increased dramatically over the years. The first improvement that I noticed was the building of a second Blackwall Tunnel in 1967. Believe it or not, the old 1897 passage under the Thames was two-way for seventy years. The Dartford Tunnel had appeared in 1963, so that helped the flow of traffic from Essex to Kent a great deal. Dartford got a second, parallel tunnel in 1980, which was splendid. However, at each of these events, the morning and evening rush hour problem more or less disappeared, but quickly returned. When the QE2 Bridge was built in 1991, we all learned the new title 'The Dartford Crossing' and within no time at all, the jams returned. This is not helped by the persistence with the toll booths, which still stop the long-suffering traffic in both directions to grab their money after all these years. Disgraceful.

The infamous M25 motorway or London Orbital (or M25 car park) was officially opened in October 1986 by Prime Minister Margaret Thatcher. Many years before this, I had been stopped and interviewed on entering the Blackwall Tunnel. All motorists were pulled up and asked a series of questions including where they were going and how often they made the journey. In hindsight, I realised that this was to do with the planned construction of the M25. A more difficult, but useful question would have been to ask (the whole of southern England) whether we thought we would use a ring road around London, because as soon as it opened, it jammed. Talk about 'build it and they will come'.

I succeeded in getting to the office in London for many years, without allowing the dreadful traffic problem to affect my morale. However, when I first started commuting, as opposed to working close to home in Kent, I felt the need to save time some other way. I immediately gave up reading newspapers, as they were a waste of my precious time. They were all becoming pretty poor in quality and, of course, a day out of date. I listened with pleasure to BBC Radios Four and Five in order to get up-to-date news and sport. This also saved watching too much television and freed up time for the family. It was very nice to listen to several presenters on Five Live, like Simon Mayo and Peter Allen, who are Spurs fans like me!

Another small, but significant daily time-saver was not having to spend any time on my hair! As a boy, it was a monthly, very short cut by my dad or a barber and I always had a neat little parting on the left-hand side, which I had to get straight. At university it was a shaggy black mop for three years. At work, it became a neat, business-like trim with a much-combed and immaculate parting until I was forty years old. If I had been in the slightest breeze, then I was five minutes in front of the mirror trying to get the parting straight again. Then my family suggested that I simply swept my hair back so that the wind blowing into my face did not matter. I bravely gave it a try and it was great. I only combed it properly once in the morning and just pushed it back if it flopped forward. After a short while, it grew that way. It was much less work and worry. The downside was that, because I did not like going to hairdressers, due to having an itchy neck for a while, it became rather long and floppy, like a grey busby hat falling over backwards. At the age of fifty, I was working in Coldharbour Lane, Brixton, where there were several hairdressers. Some specialised in Rastafarian dreadlock styles, so I carefully opted for an innocent little, old-fashioned barber shop, where they all seemed to produce what I wanted. I could barely understand their east European accents, but did my best to chat. One day, I sat in the chair with my huge grey mop waiting for a trim and was asked a question, which I did not really grasp, but nodded in agreement for some reason. As usual, I was relaxed and distracted in the seat, while the hairdresser worked away. I gradually began to feel great clumps of hair bouncing off my shoulders, but it was some time before I looked in the mirror, in amazement. I had been given what Ruth called a 'number four', that is it was very short and spiky all over! There was some disbelief, but praise at home and Clive suggested that I simply brushed it forward, which he demonstrated on my head with one hand. It looked fine and he assured me that many smart businessmen of my age in the City of London wore their hair that way. I was pleased that the time I would spend on my hair was now reduced to zero and went to work the next day. As I entered our crowded foyer, a rather tall company director yelled across the heads of our colleagues, 'Larry, what on earth has happened to your hair?'

I was surprised that it became a great talking point for quite some time! I cannot see it changing again as it is so easy to have a number four every month, especially as Ruth cuts it. Splendid.

Working in London in 2006, we had a chart on the wall for recording famous personalities we had seen, for example, I spotted Ricky Gervais in Covent Garden. Now Ricky has produced the best comedy material that I have ever seen, so I scurried after him for an autograph. He was walking quite fast with a kind of waddle, as in some of his television parts, but I caught up with him and called his name. I was most impressed. When I asked for his autograph, he politely guided me to one side, so that pedestrians could pass on the narrow pavement and asked what I would like him to write. I asked him to send good wishes to my son Clive, which he did. I won the spot-the-personality competition and my son, also a big fan, got a great autograph. Together with his pal Stephen Merchant, Ricky was responsible for the award-winning television series The Office. I must say that, in my opinion, that sitcom is up there with Fawlty Towers and the first six episodes of Rowan Atkinson's Blackadder. Ricky and Stephen's next effort, Extras, is just as good with their Christmas Special being my all-time favourite piece of television comedy. Incidentally, Pride and Prejudice with the exceptional acting skills of Colin Firth and Jennifer Ehle remains the best period drama I have ever seen. I am pleased that it remained faithful to Jane Austen's book.

Around that time I was temporarily travelling to work in London by coach, which I conveniently picked up close to my house in Rainham, Kent. I took this opportunity to read all the classic and other recommended books on a list I had compiled, so the time was by no means wasted. The coach dropped me at the Embankment and I had to walk to Drury Lane. One morning, I was crossing the usual roads, when a lady placed her foot in front of mine just as I stepped off the kerb. I had both hands free, as I used a small rucksack as a briefcase. My hands went up to break my fall as my head rushed towards the road surface. My nose and forehead just touched the ground. I leapt to my feet, of course, as though nothing had happened. I touched my nose and saw blood on my fingers, but hurried on to work. An inspection in the mirror at work showed a blooded split the length of my nose, which looked both ghastly and ridiculous. I spent the day in meetings, explaining the hideous nose, developing a headache and rejecting suggestions that I went home.

That evening I showed Ruth the damage. Obviously, she spotted it first. I could not think what to do, as a huge, long plaster would look equally silly and be uncomfortable. She, of course, had a solution and suggested a substance that would hide the cut and heal the wound. I went to Boots and was directed to certain shelves, which turned out to be full of ladies' make-up! It is the first and only time that I have bought and worn such products, but it was ideal and hid the cut almost completely.

There was, I suppose, a worse incident. I fall very infrequently, despite going out running most days, but it can hurt, particularly at speed. I tended to run around London at lunchtime, if I had time. On one occasion, I decided on a twelve mile run during an extended lunch break. I needed to run from Holborn to the far side of Hyde Park and back in a certain time in order to have a shower and go straight into a meeting. All went well until I reached the far corner of Hyde Park, where I tripped over a speed bump and went flat on my hands, elbows, knees and shins in front of a bench full of elderly ladies. I sprang up and ran off covered in blood. My hands, one elbow, both knees and one shin were scraped raw, but I ran the six miles back to work, aware of many stares. I nipped into the shower and washed off much of the blood. Having dried myself as best as I could, I began embalming the bleeding areas with copious amounts of toilet paper. It worked so well that I was able to attend two meetings without anybody realising the mess that I was in. They could not see that I was holding a thick pad of paper against the palm of each hand. I look upon it as a kind of failure, if I do not go to work and do my job due to what I consider to be a minor problem. Now that I am retired I can look back and say that I am glad that I always had a positive attitude to my job. I did not enjoy everything I did, but somebody was paying me and they deserved to have me come into work every day.

Those lunchtime runs in London were a real bonus. I am a Londoner and very proud of it, so it was great to run along the Thames and cross the bridges or to nip up to Regents Park and have a free look at the wolves as I ran past the zoo. On one occasion, I was in the very pleasant St James's Park and spotted the pelicans lined up in an ungainly manner on a narrow fence beside the lake. There were also some Japanese tourists approaching them rather timidly with cameras poised. I thought it would be amusing to brush my arm gently under the chest of the nearest pelican to see whether it would perch on my arm. It duly obliged and our overseas visitors were ecstatic, going away absolutely delighted with their photographs.

Back to the serious side of my job. Although I spent many years managing the automation of business systems, a major part of the success of any project is regular communication, that is informing and motivating the people involved in making it successful. Another key ingredient is the recruitment and training of the highest calibre staff for each task. A really good employee is worth several who are just not up to the job. I also believe that I managed to get the best out of the staff that I inherited when I sometimes picked up new responsibilities. I have managed to obtain some first class people over the years and some of them, unlike me, are now millionaires. Having talented, hard-working staff made my project management role so much easier, as well as giving me the pleasure of working with them every day.

I once took over an Information Technology team, which included a rather quiet fellow called Tom. I was very surprised one day when he did not turn up for work and made no telephone call to me either. He actually rang the next day to tell me that he had been burgled and was very shaken up, but would be in the following day to explain more fully. Well, Ruth and I had been burgled once and were not particularly bothered, so I wondered why he needed two days off. The next day Tom explained that he and his wife had been fast asleep in bed, when they had the shock of their lives to find two huge men in their bedroom. On the plus side, they were policemen. 'Sorry to surprise you sir, but a neighbour called us. He happened to wake in the night and could see you being burgled. As your front door was open, we came inside to investigate.' Naturally, Tom and his wife were quite shaken. It seems that the thieves had forced open the front door, spotted the car keys, loaded the vehicle with Tom's valuables and driven off. It was indeed a nasty shock for him and a valuable lesson for the rest of us not to leave our keys in too obvious a place. Chewing it over with Tom, I did mention my own philosophy when I am done a bad deed or unfairly dealt with in some way. I try not to be too upset, as no bad guy is going to make me feel bad. Being unkind is his problem, not mine.

I was not permanently trapped by commuting and working in an office, as business trips were fairly frequent, both within and outside the UK. I would be asked to investigate the ways that certain business issues were tackled in places like the United States and Europe. I enjoy long-haul flights and love visiting America, whether it is business or pleasure. One trip took me to New Orleans and Jackson in Louisiana. Before we went to the jazz bars in New Orleans, we checked into our really luxurious hotel. We did not mind the wait, but it took rather a long time as all the delegates for a convention for the blind were also checking in at the same time. I really admired their independence, but the process certainly had its challenges. There were dozens of them and their only sighted help were their guide dogs, which were scattering their excrement around the marble floor of the huge foyer during the chaos at the reception desk. Nobody was telling anyone when it was their turn to be served, so there was much confusion. The few staff occasionally tried to communicate, but the noise level was pretty high. Those that successfully achieved the check-in were trying to locate the lifts, but had not made it through the long, complex glass walls, which had only occasional doorways into the rest of the building. My colleague and I felt obliged to get some doors opened and politely offered to guide guests through towards the lifts. Their attitude and humour was first rate and very refreshing in a potentially stressful situation. We entered an elevator and a dozen or so unsighted guests tried to get in too, some with dogs, but we all cracked jokes and laughed at the situation. In order to avoid some of the confusion, I attempted climbing some rather narrow stairs a little later, but had to smile as two blind delegates with dogs were coming down towards me! Once my colleagues and I had settled in our bedrooms, it was somewhat strange to hear scratching noises around the doors as our fellow guests felt for their room numbers, which were also in Braille. We sighted folk have really got nothing to grumble about compared to how well and how cheerfully our blind friends cope.

The following week, I was attending a business course in Jackson with American colleagues and two lady guests from a local school. They were teachers invited to experience some of the processes occurring in industry. They were very nice, friendly women, who ended up giving us all little presents on the last day. There were sweets and so on made by their younger pupils, which was very touching, and we all had hugs and kisses, when they departed. Imagine my horror, when back in England two weeks later, I saw on our television news that there had been a fatal shooting at their school. I suppose that it is an unfortunate sign of the times that I am becoming less surprised by that sort of happening nowadays. Whilst in one of the seminars in Jackson, a lady delegate said she was a part-time policewoman. Somebody asked whether she was carrying a gun and she admitted that she 'had one with her'. She added that her son was a policeman and he carried three guns. She explained that cops can be mugged for their most obvious gun, so many tuck an extra one down the back of their pants. In case he somehow lost that too, her son had a third, smaller gun in his sock!

It was really good to invite new friends from the States to our home in Kent. Two particular pals of mine were Bill and Mary, a great couple in their sixties. He was a retired president of a well-known New York bank and she was the curator of a famous museum in that city. They also owned an island. Fortunately they loved our rather modest home and garden, in particular my aviary full of colourful budgerigars and my dovecote complete with plump babies they could hold. They asked us to show them round Charles Dickens' haunts, as these are all local to us in Kent. Part of our tour, which happened to be 4th July or Independence Day in the USA, was spent in Rochester. They were flying the American Stars and Stripes flag from the castle and when Bill saw it, he was absolutely thrilled. He also shed a tear or two.

I have been most fortunate to meet and work with some genuine and interesting people. I am pleased to say that many are still my good friends.

-12-

HOW TO SUCCEED IN LIFE BY REALLY TRYING

'And yet don't look too good, nor talk too wise'
(If by Rudyard Kipling, 1910)

Something that makes me very happy is the feeling that I am comfortable with myself. I believe that I have come to understand my behaviour and that of others, so that we can interact more harmoniously and positively.

We are not born with everything we need for success and happiness and many people never manage to acquire those attributes. Few receive any constructive feedback to help improve their behaviour and performance. Also, much of what we give and receive is of a negative nature, telling us what not to do. It tends to stem from childhood, when we are frequently told 'no'. It is much more useful to advise or coach a child or adult in how to go forward confidently.

I was fortunate during my working life to have a number of excellent bosses. Some of these were instrumental in my personal development as well as work-related skills. Project management and the development of staff were always among my strong points, so on one particular occasion it was interesting to hear my boss's view on what I needed next. He told me that I had all the technical skills that I needed to do the job, so the next step was to further develop my interpersonal skills. This was the start of some important self-development, which positively affected my behaviour both at work and at home. I was fortunate to have a manager with that insight and skill to help me.

I have discovered one thing though. There's a lot more you can learn, if you are prepared to listen. This, of course, is the first thing to master; how to really listen, but there is the initial question 'Why do we need to listen?' Listening is extremely important to all of us in order to understand and learn. Learning to me is motivational and a pleasure in itself. There are several levels of listening and my explanation of this is as follows:

Let us start at the lowest level, which is 'not listening'. At this level you hear nothing, learn nothing, can add no value and are more or less wasting your time. It may be of some comfort to the speaker, but not if they realise that you are not really there. Let us say that a friend or colleague is trying to tell you something, for example why they are late for work, and you are just not taking it in. You learn nothing and are of no real help at all.

Now, move up the levels a bit. This is where you are listening, but simply in order to agree or disagree with what is being said. Many of us are just waiting to say yes or no. You could agree that the traffic was bad enough to make him late or tell him that it was not that bad and he should get up earlier. You haven't really explored his problem at all, but may feel satisfied that you passed an opinion.

Let us move up to another level, where you are listening in order to jump in and tell your own story about your traffic problem and why you were once late. You have given him no chance to elaborate, you have not helped or understood and you have learned nothing. You could tell this same story of yours again and again to many people with little merit.

So let us try a slightly higher level where we are listening attentively, but only to obtain information useful to ourselves. Our responses to the speaker are usually quite mechanical and detached. At this stage, in the traffic example, we may be thinking of how we might use that information to our own advantage when travelling home that evening and avoid being late.

Moving up the levels a little more, we are paying a great deal of attention to the speaker, checking that we understand the points being made and actively demonstrating our interest in what they are saying. That is probably somewhat reassuring to the speaker, but little more.

The final stage is to try to have none of the above thoughts, but to relax the mind and get a feel for what is being said. The listener becomes aware of the speaker's feelings and emotions, developing a real empathy. Maybe the lateness was nothing to do with traffic, maybe there is a deeper, perhaps personal problem that you could help solve once you understand what is really being said. So, why we really need to listen is to understand, learn and help. The solution may not be criticism, analysis or answers, but just letting them speak. If it's your partner, they might just need a hug.

Another important skill is the ability to focus. This is where you have your mind and body in the same place at the same time. You are not at work thinking about home and you are not at home thinking about work, which can both be unproductive and worrying. I suppose, even worse, you could be driving home thinking about work and not noticing the traffic around you!

I know some folk who go back and check that they have properly closed their front door several times, because they were not clearly focussed on what they were doing, but perhaps on what they will do next. This behaviour often extends to the workplace, where lack of concentration does little for the quality of your work, your career or job satisfaction. If you are going to be at work for the same eight hours as everybody else, why not focus on your work, do it effectively and enhance your career? If you have done a good job, you should not need to worry about it at home. If you have been kind and helpful to your partner at home, then you can go to work with a clear conscience and concentrate there too.

In a similar way, some sportsman start thinking about things that did not work the last time they tried something, like beating another player, and, whilst they are worrying about that, they lose their focus and it goes wrong again.

The problem with all these examples is that the people concerned are less than happy with their lot. They are either wasting time or underperforming or both. We may need to practise this focussing by setting a simple goal and executing it. You could be writing a report at work, and when you finish, go home with a clear conscience and concentrate on the family. You could, say, make a list of jobs at home, start tackling them and go to work without them on your mind. You could be first to cross that line by just focussing on the finish, running your fastest and nothing else matters. You are tackling that winger and will get the ball. You are shutting that door and it is shut.

Something else that we all need at various times in our business and private lives is the ability to deal with the changes that continuously bombard us. Do you, for example, ever find yourself reacting negatively to changes at work or home? Of course you do. Most of us do. Can you remember a change turning out well, but you had not been prepared to see any positives in it at first? Maybe you had a new boss or a new item bought by your partner for the home and you were initially quite sceptical, but they turned out better than expected? It has happened to me more than once! If we did not go along with some changes, we would not make progress, so it is often worthwhile suspending judgement until you know a little more about it. If it is just a suggestion, you may even be able to build on the idea yourself and ensure it turns out well, if you keep an open mind and listen.

Have you ever been frustrated by the behaviour of a boss or partner, because it is different to how you would do things? Have you decided that they will never change? You cannot necessarily change other people, so maybe you should change the way you approach them, if you want a good result. Try to understand their style and use the strength of it, whilst complementing it with your own, different skills. If, for example, they are naturally dogmatic, you may need to be more persuasive, assertive and constructive, offering win-win solutions. If you both gain, then you could have a workable way forward.

Do you ever waste time and energy ranting about things that you cannot change, like the weather? Do you ever moan about things that you think you cannot change, like a broken computer printer at work? How much time and energy is spent complaining instead of doing? Why not walk round the corner to that IT department and ask somebody to please make sure the printer gets fixed? Make a list of quick wins and get on with them. You will feel good and look good.

> God grant me the serenity to accept the things I cannot change;
> courage to change the things I can;
> and wisdom to know the difference.

It is well known that most people do not like change. It can make you feel uncomfortable or insecure, but it can also be interesting and refreshing. There is a 'change exercise' where you all enter a room and sit where you like, then after a while you are all asked to sit somewhere else, next to a different person. At first it seems odd, then rather more interesting, then completely comfortable. Personally, I noticed that when I went to a restaurant with my wife, I always sat with my back to the wall, where I could face everybody. My wife therefore only saw me, poor thing. After that seat-changing exercise, I made a point of inviting Ruth to sit looking 'outwards' and I faced her. I now do this whenever possible, as I can concentrate on her and what she is saying. She can either look around or put up with me, but women can multi-process anyway or so I am told.

Another thing that made a great difference to my life was understanding accountability. Why will nobody answer that phone over there? It may be a customer. Why will nobody fix the computer printer that we all share? But that phone and that printer are not your responsibility, or are they?

What's the difference between accountability and responsibility? Take the example of a football team, who have just spent six million pounds on a new left back. His responsibility is clearly to defend that left side from attack. He may also have been told to push forward when possible and help his strikers. Now, what does he do when his centre back colleague falls over during an opposition attack down the middle? Does he say that it is nothing to do with him? I think we all know that he will run across and cover the centre for the good of the team. He knows his job description and his responsibility, but he also feels accountable for the team's results and will help out at all times. To cap it all, wouldn't it be great, if he saw the opportunity, to dash forward and smash in a winning goal for his team? How good does that feel?

This introduces the subject of teamwork. I have worked for companies where certain departments refused to cooperate with one another. No wonder that their competitors won the customers. I know of families who do not pull together, whereas most households benefit enormously from being part of 'the team'.

Whether at work, at play or at home, why not think this simple thought 'What else can I do to help?' I love the whole idea. Some years ago, after thinking about accountability and teamwork, I decided to do all the washing up at home, since Ruth did all the cooking. I actually enjoy the process. It may seem like a small start, but I now enjoy helping others in any way that I can. It is a pleasure not a chore.

You can look at accountability another way. We sometimes feel powerless, let down or stitched up, when things go badly, but, wait a minute, we were there, so what did we do? What could we have done differently? What will we do next time? The outcome of many situations could be up to you, not fate or other people, so take action. You will feel much happier if you have some control.

I learned to plan at a young age, but the ability to prioritise tasks took a bit longer. I have read that one of the greatest causes of stress, after bereavement and moving house, is a lack of planning or time management.

I have a solution, but, unless you know me and my diary, you will probably think it is 'over the top'. In order to achieve all the large and small things I need for myself and others, I plan them out in my pocket diary. I get great satisfaction from the act of doing this, feel completely in control and get most things achieved.

Planning can be as simple as jotting down a to-do list and ticking off the things that you complete. Anything not achieved can be quickly assessed and moved forward a day or more, as appropriate. I use my pocket diary for all of this and have all sorts of work and pleasure mapped out in it, along with birthdays, anniversaries and football matches. In fact, it contains any task of any magnitude that will help keep my life sane and smooth. I am not keen on making mistakes and this minimises that risk. It's great and I feel relaxed and happy every time I tick things off.

As I mentioned earlier in my story, we once had a baby and moved house just after I changed my job. It was not stressful, because we made a project out of it. The technique has been called 'gap analysis and action planning', whereby you look at where you are now, where you need to be and the actions or tasks required to get there. On a grander scale this is project management, providing you can determine all the critical tasks and hit your deadlines, preferably within budget. This usually requires a fair amount of relevant, targeted communication to be successful. I'm not sounding very spontaneous, but within an overall framework, I try to achieve things in a different, more relaxed style at home!

Prioritising is really about picking out the tasks that are really important and doing those first. When you look at your work for the day or even your emails, it is tempting to start by picking off the easy items, often at the expense of key things that really must be done. I think we can fairly quickly assess what must be done first, if we stop and think for a little while.

When I was a boy, I remember my dad looking in a little pocket diary, where he also tucked pieces of paper. At the time I did not know why he did this, but I have been doing it myself for over forty years. It is another thing for which I thank him. My son's pocket diary is electronic and it works for him. I can certainly see his daughter doing the same thing, as she already appreciates the benefits of being well-organised and in control of her life.

Something that many people must accept, whether they are famous or simply parents, is that, like it or not, we become role models for others. How we behave is key to the way others behave, especially our children or staff at work. Have you ever had a disorganised boss who is running around like a headless chicken? However hard some of their staff may try, the result is often that they are equally disorganised. They may even assume that it is normal behaviour, so it is okay to emulate it. If, however, he or she installs some planning and systems, then folk will equally tend to follow that lead.

Have you ever encountered an aggressive boss with equally aggressive subordinates or an unpleasant father or mother with rude children? It is our responsibility to behave in such a way that sets a good example. We all, I included, need to think about the things we do and make sure there is consistency with what we say.

Some of the worst examples of bad role models or even hypocrisy involves people in high places, like certain corrupt politicians, immoral clergymen or policemen and judges who break the law. Unfortunately for our impressionable children, we see many unsporting sportsmen. I am quite horrified yet fascinated by surly barmen or bad service in restaurants. Do they not realise that you are a customer on their premises, paying to enjoy yourself? BREAKING NEWS: many of our MPs have been allegedly fiddling their expenses (May 2009, if you could ever forget). UPDATE: a large number of MPs and cabinet ministers are standing down. What a shower. Not all of them, just the greedy, pompous ones, who forgot why they were elected or suffered from a false sense of superiority. Let the good role models step forward please.

On the positive side, another step we could take is to coach other people, especially those younger than ourselves, to improve their behaviour or performance. You may have seen that exercise where a blindfolded person is asked to throw soft balls into a wastepaper basket, but they do not know where it is. It gets worse when he or she misses and they hear laughter and jeering. It gets better when somebody acts as a coach and offers verbal guidance, like telling them in which direction to throw and how hard. After a little more coaching, they are successful, onlookers cheer and the 'victim' smiles. You may have started a job in the dark and been chastised for your mistakes, but not praised for good work. This is a plea for setting people in the right direction, including children, and telling them, constructively, what they should be doing, how they are getting on and how to improve even further. Children hear 'no' much more often than 'yes' or 'maybe' and I believe this stays with them for life. It is better to give children choices rather than yes or no options. It is that old trick of saying, 'Which hand do you want to hold, this one or that one?' instead of 'Hold my hand now!' It sounds simplistic, but it may work.

I suppose it is more advising than coaching, but it is also a good idea to sit with someone and tell them three things that you really appreciate about them and one thing that you could help them to change or improve. It is essential that this is constructive, showing a way forward, and you must ask their permission to give feedback in the first place. Then ask them to do the same for you. No, it is not embarrassing or a bit 'twee', give it a try.

Perhaps all these things come naturally to some folk, but I have had to learn and develop most of them, which has given me much enjoyment and satisfaction.

- 13 -

COMMITTEES

'A committee is a group that keeps minutes and loses hours.'
(Milton Berle, 1960)

I seem to have been on a lot of committees. This is probably because I enjoy organising various activities and generally helping to get things done. When we moved into our present home in 1972, the twenty-six houses in the close contained forty children. As I mentioned earlier, our neighbours had formed a sports and social club with sections for football, art and drama. There were also many special events and activities for the growing band of kids. We had an overall club committee and sub-committees for the sections. I had various spells as chairman, treasurer and secretary, enjoying it all. Another task was editing our magazine Close-Up, where I had a gardening column called 'The Rake'. All of this lasted for many years and, although the structure has disappeared, we are still good friends. As I sit upstairs writing this book, my three closest sets of original neighbours are all still in residence. I must give special mention to the best neighbours in the world, John and Janet. It always feels good to know that they are next door and not just because Jan looks after my house and garden while we are away!

When the children started at primary school, I joined the Parent Teachers Association or PTA and soon took over as chairman. I felt that I should take an interest in my children's schooling and this was pretty hands-on, what with the traditional fund-raising jumble sales and dances.

After thirty years, we still socialise regularly with very good friends made on that committee, namely Dick, Trisha, David, Sandra and Mick.

I also became an elected school governor and got to meet the head and staff more often. In this way I came to understand the ethos of the school. The governing body had a surprising composition, including representatives from the main political parties and the local vicar. Having parent governors like me was a fairly new idea. One decision I remember very well was that children could bring packed lunches, if they did not want school dinners. I was against this, as I thought they would bring junk food. I preferred the camaraderie and discipline of sitting down in the restaurant and eating what you were given, which seemed to be nourishing food. At the next governors' meeting, the head teacher reported that the take-up of packed lunches was much higher than expected. She was worried about the economic viability of the restaurant. I had previously argued that if you give them all the choice, they may take the one you do not want. At the next meeting, our head reported a significant problem with litter from the packed lunches and her horror at the poor quality food that pupils were bringing from home. Well, many things start as the thin end of a wedge.

On a lighter note, we had many jumble sales and some of the first car boot fairs held in Britain. I personally made over £50 from my first boot stall, which was an incredibly useful sum of money in 1978. A very handy gentleman known as Mr White always took away the unwanted and broken goods after every jumble sale. He arrived early one day, so I stood chatting to him for a while. He revealed that he had fourteen children and one on the way. So far it was nine boys, all named after darts players apparently, and five girls. He told me, with a glint in his eye, that if the next one was a girl, he favoured Isla as a name. I thought at first it was because Larry Grayson's assistant on his popular game show, the Generation Game, was Isla St Clair. But no, a few weeks later, there was Mr W on the front page of the local newspaper with baby number fifteen, Isla White.

Most of the primary school classes had a pet, like a guinea pig, gerbil or mouse. A friend told me a great little story about their school's small rodents. In their daughter's classroom was a cage containing two baby mice. They were what you call 'fancy' pet mice as opposed to wild ones. The teacher had specifically asked for two little females, so that they would not breed. A number of weeks went by and some babies were born. The teacher was cross and asked a colleague, who understood how to tell the sex of a mouse, what was going on. The colleague reported that they were both definitely female and one must have been pregnant when purchased, despite being just a youngster itself. Other interested folk refuted that and something of a mystery evolved, especially when, a few days later, the other female gave birth. The teacher had a lot of babies to re-house, but, once done, that should have been the end of the problem. A month or so later, to her horror, the teacher found that both mice had given birth to another litter, even though they had not left the cage. A debate ensued as to whether a mouse can be impregnated as a baby with multiple future litters! It was decided that this was not the case. The possibility that a little male from the first litter was responsible was ruled out as they were given away whilst sexually immature. Everyone was sure that the bars of the cage were far too narrow for a mouse to get in or out. One evening, a teacher decided to sit and quietly watch the cage to see what might happen. After a while she spotted a scrawny little field mouse come into the classroom via a hole in the skirting. He could not get through the bars of the cage, but ran round the back. Soon he was inside the cage attending to both females. The alarmed teacher ran to the cage and saw him off. She delved into every corner of the cage, moving small lumps of sawdust and there was the answer. Our romantic little friend had chewed a tiny hole in a rear, dark corner of a strong wooden cage to find the girls. Some time later I began to wonder how many homes and pet shops in the area housed these rather cute little mixed race mice.

My children took their turns to look after classroom pets during school holidays and we had quite a variety. This was when I encountered stick insects for the first time. They were long thin greenish-brown creatures that moved very slowly and merged with twigs on plants so that they were hard to spot. They came to us in an escape-proof box with a transparent lid and we kept them in the kitchen until the next school term started. The babies were tiny and we were careful not to let them escape, which seemed easy enough, until the box was returned to the classroom. Now, in our kitchen was a waste bin with a trailing plant above it. I began to notice what appeared to be mouse droppings around the bin, which was a bit disturbing, but we could not see any other signs of mice. I cleaned up these small black specs every day. It was many days before I started staring at this trailing plant as if transfixed by something. I eventually detected a giant, well-camouflaged, very slow-moving stick insect grazing happily on the leaves. At the next school meeting, I presented them with the largest creature in their collection.

I was also a governor at both my children's secondary schools. Some of the highlights included forming sub-committees to select new head teachers, which was both a fascinating and disappointing process, as there never seemed to be any candidates of the same high quality as the outgoing heads.

Whilst vice-chairman of the governors at my son's school, we had the idea of setting up a Disciplinary Panel to give a last chance to those boys about to be 'expelled' from the school for misconduct. It was an unusual school insomuch as it contained both grammar and non-grammar streams, known as bilateral. It was an all boys school with the usual crimes and punishment. There was no extreme violence, drug-taking or knives, but bullying and class disruption were significant problems. The trouble with expulsion or permanent exclusion, as we came to call it, was that the excluded boys simply rotated from school to school. You would get rid of one and a worse one would be sent to replace him. We were once offered an arsonist in exchange for a bully, but chose not to take him. I left the problem with the local authority, which had closed the special units that used to take such children. We decided to give those boys facing exclusion one last chance to change their ways. They would appear before a panel of three governors and agree to sign a contract outlining the required change in behaviour. They had to be accompanied by their parents or guardian and we would discuss the problems before getting down to an agreed way forward. The contract itself would be signed by me, as chairman of the panel, the headmaster, the boy and a parent or guardian. I must say that many a parent did their poor sons no favours with their own attitudes and behaviour. One father appeared at a meeting with an aggressive slogan emblazoned on his pullover and claimed that all kids fight. He said he was sure that I got into fights at school, so it was natural and not a problem. I pointed out that I actually did not, but we were there to discuss his boy, not me. Some parents would claim that a certain teacher did not like their child and picked on him, until I pointed out that several different teachers had written many pages about their lad's poor behaviour. I felt sorry for nearly all the boys I saw and only found myself actually disliking one or two. We always got the signatures and a good percentage never re-offended. Most that ignored our agreement were subsequently excluded for the good of the children wishing to learn.

Now that I am in my sixties, I realise that I have not been on any kind of committee for some years and that is fine. All these activities need fresh blood, but I am pleased to have done my bit and learned a great deal along the way.

- 14 -

DYLAN, BEATLES, STONES, OASIS …

'If music be the food of love, play on; give me excess of it'
(Twelfth Night by William Shakespeare, 1601)

I do like music very much, without needing it constantly available. The first record that I owned was 'Positively 4th Street' by Bob Dylan. Ruth bought it for me in September 1965, because I liked Dylan's words. I realised that it was the first present I had received without it being my birthday or Christmas. As Ruth and I were to marry three years later, it was a very poignant gift.

Ruth was a big fan of popular music before I cottoned on. She would listen to Radio Luxemburg on her little transistor radio under her bedclothes, when her parents thought she was asleep. My sister Colleen had pictures of Elvis everywhere (and still does) but music did not really interest me in my early teens. Ruth bought the New Musical Express (NME) magazine and voted each year in their polls for best solo artist, best group etc. She attended her first NME Poll Winners Concert in 1964 and I accompanied her on 11th April 1965 at the Empire Pool, Wembley. The tickets cost twenty-five shillings each (one pound and twenty-five pence), but the line-up was unbelievable. Imagine being able to see, in one live concert, the Beatles, the Rolling Stones, the Hollies, the Searchers, Herman's Hermits, the Kinks, the Animals, Them, the Moody Blues, Tom Jones, Dusty Springfield, Cilla Black, Donovan, the Rockin' Berries, Sounds Incorporated, Freddie and the Dreamers, Georgie Fame and the

Blue Flames, Wayne Fontana and the Mindbenders, the Seekers, the Ivy League and the Bachelors. Just read that again, as if the Beatles and Stones were not enough. These were not tribute bands!

It was on 5th October 2000 at Wembley Arena that I eventually saw Dylan perform live in Britain. I went with my son, a most enthusiastic and knowledgeable music fan, and to my surprise the audience was full of youngsters. Two lads sitting behind us were talking admiringly about John Lennon. I decided it would be OK to just turn round and tell them that I had seen him perform live. They were so pleased and just wanted to talk about it. It's amazing how that great music lives on.

Ruth and I have been to New York several times and, of course, visited the spot where John Lennon was murdered. It is the Dakota apartment building, which was John and Yoko Ono's home until he was shot by Mark Chapman on 8th December 1980. The Strawberry Fields memorial was established in memory of Lennon in nearby Central Park.

My son loves Indie (independent) music and spotted the band Oasis in their very early days. On 22nd July 2000, Clive and I went to see them at Wembley Stadium. Both Gallagher brothers were there and they played all their great hits, so it was tremendously exciting. We left our seats and spent the whole concert jumping up and down right in front of the stage. It was terrific. It is quite fascinating, having seen all these acts, that the Gallaghers were influenced by the Beatles, who had admired the work of Dylan, who had started to imitate Buddy Holly and so it goes on.

Probably the two best performers I have seen on stage are Chuck Berry and Rod Stewart. Their movement and music was fantastic. They were really exciting times. As it happens, Rod Stewart attended the same secondary school as my sister Colleen. This was the William Grimshaw School in Muswell Hill, where their contemporaries were Ray and Dave Davies of the Kinks. The Davies brothers lived in Denmark Terrace not far from our house and had six sisters. The school music teacher asked them to get together and play something for the school dance, so that is how they started. They had other names, like the Ravens, before somebody suggested that they were different or kinky, so their famous name came into being. Many music buffs believe that the Kinks great hit 'You Really Got Me' was absolutely ground-breaking and influenced many future performers right up to today.

Another great artist is Elton John, who we saw in concert at the Royal Albert Hall, but he probably gave his greatest and bravest performance at Princess Diana's funeral in Westminster Abbey in 1997. Elton's remake of

Candle in the Wind, commencing Goodbye England's Rose, sold thirty-seven million copies, topping the charts in the UK, the USA, Germany, Japan and many other countries.

If I may digress from music for a while, Diana died on 31st August 1997, five days before another much loved lady, Mother Teresa, passed away in Calcutta. It was a Sunday on which Diana was killed and on the following day I dropped Ruth in London for one of her summer holiday walkabouts, while I was at work. It was early morning when she went to Kensington Palace and observed just two bouquets at the gates, which we all know quickly swelled to over a million. By the statue of Peter Pan in Kensington Gardens, there was a single rose and we have a photograph of that scene on the wall at home. Back in 1992, we had visited India and seen one of Mother Teresa's missions in Delhi before moving on to visit the Taj Mahal in Agra. We sat where Diana also sat for that famous, sad, iconic picture, which made her unhappiness rather public. So, five years later, at her funeral, I do not know how Elton got through that lovely haunting song. Not many people could have done that.

In recent years, we were pleased to see Joe Brown and Paul Jones. Ruth had seen them both at the 1964 NME Poll Concert, when Joe led The Bruvvers and Paul was with Manfred Mann. They were as good as ever. They still had their voices and looks too! In my humble opinion, Paul is a terrific singer and the best harmonica player of all time.

It is June 2009 and I have just seen Neil Sedaka on television promoting his new CD and tour. He is seventy this year and still sings beautifully. Ruth and I saw him in concert some ten years ago, when he performed twenty-five terrific songs. I counted them at the time, as I was fascinated by the sheer quality of what we were hearing. Incidentally, he has been married to the same lady since 1962, which sits well with me, and seems to be an extremely agreeable fellow too. Good luck to him.

There are many songs that I have really enjoyed over a span of about forty-six years, but I feel that I must mention some favourites that give me a feeling of real pleasure. My first is that haunting ballad 'Danny Boy', which was written in 1910 by a Somerset born Oxford graduate named Frederick Weatherly. It is rather nice that I now have a little grandson named Daniel. My second is 'When you were sweet sixteen' by an Irish band The Fureys, as the meaningful words remind me of meeting Ruth. We are both very fond of Barry White's immortal song 'The First, the Last, My Everything' and play it frequently.

I am aware that a big hit when I was born in 1947 in our capital city was 'Maybe it's because I'm a Londoner' by the splendid Bud Flanagan, so I have a quiet affection for that song too. As usual, I discover a little coincidence, which is that Bud's parents lived in Brick Lane, east London, close to my great grandparents.

Like many people, I enjoy the Elvis classics like 'Are you lonesome tonight?' Also, many of Rod Stewart's tracks are on my list of favourite songs, especially 'I don't want to talk about it' and 'Maggie May', but I suppose that I most frequently go back to Dylan's 'Positively 4th Street', my first record. It has the most unusual words, it swings along as well as anything ever written and Ruth bought it for me.

In October 2009, Ruth and I visited Liverpool with our good friends Nick and Linda. In addition to being entertained in the new Cavern Club in Mathew Street, we did the tour of John Lennon and Paul McCartney's homes, which I would recommend to anyone. They are owned by the National Trust and decorated as they were in 1957, when sixteen-year-old John met Paul, aged just fifteen. Apart from the memories of the Beatles and seeing where they composed their first big hits, waves of nostalgia swept over me at the sight of all that nineteen-fifties furniture and décor. My childhood was mirrored there. Both lads slept in the 'box rooms' overlooking their front gardens, as I did. John also played 'cowboys and indians', which was my favourite activity as a child. They were obviously musically gifted and I am not, but I did tap out a little tune on the upright piano in Paul's parents' front room.

Ruth's mum and dad had spent a short while in Liverpool in the 1930s and their son David was born there. When I first met him, Syd would sometimes refer to Ruth as Judy, a Liverpudlian name for a girl or girlfriend. Well, I can say with great pleasure, 'Hey Jude'.

-15-

SAD AND DISTURBING TIMES

'Live as if you were to die tomorrow. Learn as if you were to live forever'
(Mahatma Ghandi, 1910)

I have, of course, had some very sad moments, which have mostly been bereavements. After the initial shock and sadness, my reaction is to try to see where I can help make things a little better and take away some of the pain. I suppose that my generally pragmatic nature comes to the fore. I know that memories of unhappy and potentially depressing incidents will enter my head and I cannot prevent that, but I do not let them stay too long. As well as taking some constructive action, I try my best to think and speak about that person or event in more positive and happier terms.

As you get older, the number of deaths and funerals you attend seems to increase dramatically. Several guys that I worked with have passed away, mostly around my age, but some a fair bit younger. I know that stress affected some of them and smoking cigarettes was clearly a factor in several cases too. Among my friends and neighbours, I have twice attended the funerals of children. I find the loss of a child and the sight of those small coffins so deeply sad. Every man and woman cried during the services.

I do not really remember my grandparents or their deaths, as I was either not born or too young. The first major loss I can recall was Ruth's father Syd, who died in 1973. Ruth and I were on holiday on a farm in Northumberland with Clive aged one year and Ruth just pregnant again. Syd was very fond of Clive and called him the 'little chap'. It was very sad when Ruth's mum, Ethel, telephoned the farmer to tell us that Syd had died in hospital. We rang her back and she insisted that we complete our little holiday. At least we were able to tell her that Ruth was pregnant, but unfortunately Syd did not know. He had been one of the first people to have surgery and a drainage bag fitted for colitis or inflammation of the colon. Just like his earlier heart attack, he overcame this and started a new job managing a large toy shop. He was naturally very enthusiastic and very good at it. He had previously worked for Marks & Spencer and had been a director of a fruit importing firm in London's Covent Garden, travelling frequently to the Channel Islands. He was also about to open one of Britain's first self-service greengrocers, a forerunner of our supermarkets. Syd had it all planned out, when the Second World War broke out and ruined everything.

Syd was sixty-four, as was my father when we lost him a few years later. Two months before Dad's longed-for retirement he was having his gall bladder removed. It was hardly keyhole surgery in 1976 and he showed us the long, ugly scar across his stomach when we visited him with Clive and little Katy. Clive was four years old and the earliest memory of his life was seeing Dad wearing pyjamas and sitting in the hospital bed. As we left the ward, we managed to dislocate Kate's arm, presumably by pulling her along. A doctor popped it back straight away and it has stayed there ever since. The next day the hospital rang my sister to tell her that Dad had died in the night from a pulmonary embolism. She rang Ruth, who called me at work. It was a very difficult call for her to make. It was several years before I stopped dreaming that Dad was still alive. My dreams were so realistic that I would awake the following morning thinking that his death had been the dream and that he was actually still with us. I am glad that I always kissed Dad goodbye, especially that afternoon.

I am grateful to my friend Pete for his positive comment that 'At least your dad had arranged his life the way he wanted it.'

Just before Dad went into hospital for the operation, he said he would not bother to own a car when he retired and asked whether I would like to buy his Ford Capri. I agreed, as it was a nice car and a step up from my Ford Anglia. I was to give Dad £400, which I ended up giving to Mum instead. The car is worth describing, as Dad bought it following a full page advertisement in a national newspaper. Ford was producing one thousand bright orange Capris, all 2000cc. They had black vinyl roofs, black slats on the rear window and matching spoiler on the boot. Dad decided that he would prefer a 1600cc GT, so he telephoned Ford and they fitted just one of these special editions with the engine Dad desired. Trust Dad to think of that and get it. There was one little hiccup. Somewhere on the dashboard was a funny little flexible reading light, which was handy for maps. However, on a journey with our friends, Dave and Jean, smoke emerged from the glove compartment, where we found the wiring end of the gadget melting and burning. I stopped and sprung the bonnet, whilst Dave quickly found a spanner among my tools and disconnected the battery. This allowed everything to cool down until we could remove the offending item. I thought he did well to think of immediately cutting off the electricity supply like that. I sometimes wonder what I would have done, if it had happened while I was alone. Incidentally, I sold the car after only a year, as my boss wanted to tie me into the job with a pay rise and company car. However, I have a little reminder of that Capri, because I managed to obtain a model replica of that and every car that we have driven. Where necessary, I have painted them in the colours of their big brothers and all twenty-six are in a display case in the kitchen.

Ruth's mother Ethel was amazing and almost indescribable, but I will try. She was forty when Ruth was born, so I never knew her when she was young. She was short, tubby, energetic, full of love, had strong opinions on everything, wrote letters of complaint and was the sort of old lady that served dinners to elderly folk much younger than her! She contracted breast cancer in her early eighties and was completely brave and matter of fact about it. She stayed in her own home quite near to us for as long as she could, but eventually went into a hospice. Around this time we met the Macmillan nurses. Now there is a group worthy of support. They were so caring towards dear Ethel until she died peacefully on Christmas Day, as a visiting Salvation Army band played Jingle Bells. Ruth, Kate and I held her hands as she slipped away. Following the cremation, Ruth, her brother Dave, his wife Jean and I took Ethel's ashes and those of her dear husband Syd to the church in Southgate, north London, where she had worshipped and we were married. The vicar conducted a short service for us and the two urns were gently emptied into the same hole in the garden border in front of the church. Ashes to ashes.

As a footnote to this, I must mention that Dave planted a rose with an appropriate name, 'Sweethearts', above the ashes. As neither Dave and Jean nor Ruth and I tend to visit that spot in the summer, none of us had seen the rose in flower. We had all pruned it many times and planted spring bulbs around it, but it was not until 2008 that Ruth and I made a summer visit and were knocked out by the beauty of the rose. There were just two flowers, one taller than the other, but close together like Syd and Ethel. The colour was a vivid apricot and they were simply stunning. I sent Ruth's brother and wife a photograph via my telephone and they were thrilled.

My mother Lilian lived to a remarkable ninety-four, passing away in January 2008. She died from dementia in a nursing home in Folkestone. I put her long life down to walking many miles a day and not smoking. She also kept slim with a modest diet, including fruit and vegetables. Mum did not realise that she was doing all the right things for a long life, but simply behaved as she wished. Even in her eighties, she walked six times a day, amounting to some seventy miles a week, accompanied over the years by a series of rescued dogs. As she became less able, my sisters visited Mum almost every day to do the housework or deliver shopping. My brother saw Mum every week and I drove to Folkestone to be with her about once a fortnight until I retired, when I saw her more frequently.

Mum saw the doctor occasionally and he started to diagnose various illnesses for which she needed medication. First there was mild diabetes, then a weak heart, followed by a little arthritis and constipation and so it went on. Mum had a row of tablets on her coffee table, all with bold, handwritten notes on how many to take and when to take them. Added to this was a potion for indigestion, most likely caused by all these tablets. Do you begin to recognise this pattern of drugs, side effects and further medicines to counteract them? Well she became very ill and was admitted to hospital, where due to lack of attention, she got worse, weighing about six stone and unable to walk. My sisters had to visit every day, despite it being a significant driving distance, to make sure she was getting food and water. The need for regular drinks of water was actually written on her notes at the end of the bed, but nurses were just not giving her a drink. Juice and water was left by catering staff, but Mum was too weak and confused to find it. I once went in and found a full jug of water, but no beaker or straw. Sorry to go on about it, but it is important and, I believe, quite common. I requested a beaker, which came from a back room, after a search. It was a dodgy little thin plastic thing and I wondered what it had been used for previously, but I desperately needed to rehydrate my mother. Somehow, after my siblings and I all thought Mum would surely die, she rallied, improved and was discharged. I am still amazed at her recovery, but what stunned me even more was that the doctor said she was not diabetic and had a heart stronger than his own. He prescribed only one aspirin a day in the way of medication. Goodbye to all those drugs.

Although she was approaching ninety years old, we did not realise soon enough that Mum was losing her mind. When we tried to get power of attorney to help handle her affairs, we were told that she did not understand the concept, so it could not be granted.

I had to apply through the courts to become Mum's 'receiver', which is similar in practice to having power of attorney. There was a great deal of bureaucracy and I became answerable to the Court of Protection. I managed the process correctly, so they were supportive and we did everything that was required to look after Mum. Unfortunately, she became more frail and confused and needed twenty-four hour care. It was clear that we could not cope and my sisters found a suitable nursing home in the locality so that friends and family could visit her frequently. Despite the home being plain and unpretentious, it was loving and friendly. We got to know the staff and Mum's new friends very well. Nearly all the residents suffered from dementia and we found them mostly to be very sweet old folk. Colleen and Marilyn visited nearly every day with Gordon and I popping in nearly every week. I would say that Mum had the most visitors and we often got roped in to help with games and parties. It is very important to provide people in the care of these homes with regular stimulation of the mind and not to simply leave them staring into space. All of Mum's savings were used to pay for the cost of her care and we also had to sell Mum's little bungalow when the cash ran out. She was as happy there as she could be, considering that she did not really know what was going on. Mum was a very important and dear person, so I would like to reproduce here the eulogy I wrote for her funeral in January 2008, a legacy of love:

Lilian was born as Lilian Margaret Harvey on New Year's Day in 1914 in Bethnal Green, east London. She therefore lived through two World Wars.

Her father was a foreman for the GPO and she had two sisters, Edie and Doris, and a brother, John.

She said she was good at reading, writing and drawing at school and was a good runner.

In those days she was fortunate to have a bicycle and a violin, which she could play.

She started work as a milliner in east London and she must have been good, because her boss sent her to the West End to note down and copy the expensive hats on sale there. Lilian would reproduce these for sale in Bethnal Green.

She met and married Joseph Brooks in Bethnal Green. "Joe" worked as a bus driver, then at the BBC and later as an insurance agent. They had five children, one of whom, Pauline, sadly died as a baby.

The other four children, Gordon, Colleen, Larry and Marilyn are here united today.

"Mum" cared for her children in a very loving and protective way and woe betide anyone who would have tried to harm them. She also worked very hard outside the home, taking various jobs to earn extra money to help feed and clothe the "kids". She often went without to provide for her precious children.

About ten years after moving in 1967 from London to Folkestone, she lost her husband Joe, who she will soon be re-joining after 32 years.

I must also mention Mum's lovely dogs, including poodles, but mostly whippets from a rescue home. She would walk them up to 70 miles a week, even when she was in her 70's and 80's.

Mum spent the last two years of her life in the loving care of Mont Calm nursing home, who we thank enormously.

Mum liked music and singing, so you are hearing three of her favourite songs here today.

What Mum has left behind is her everlasting love for her children, and this love has been passed to her grandchildren and great-grandchildren, which makes them all very lucky to have been loved by Mum and their parents, aunties and uncles.

Thank you Mum.

I mention with great sadness the year 2005. This was a dreadful time, as both my sisters were widowed. Colleen's husband, Pat, had retired from his own building business. He battled with several serious illnesses, including Parkinson's Disease, colitis and finally cancer, but he was a good-natured chap and always greeted me unselfishly with, 'How are you?' Colleen and I held his hands as he passed away aged seventy-two. Marilyn's husband Paul was a draughtsman by trade and a good sportsman. He died suddenly at home, far too young aged fifty-four. So, I have two lovely, widowed sisters who I see as often as possible.

In between the deaths of my two brothers-in-law, we also lost somebody very close to our son in the July 7th London bombing. Members of my family and I were amongst those people running from hospital to hospital seeking news. It was quite surreal when Ruth brushed shoulders with the Queen, who was visiting the hospital, but Ruth ignored her as we were rushing to our car to continue the search. My only consolation is that she was a very caring person who enjoyed life to the full.

Although the following deaths did not directly affect our family, a terrible incident occurred back in March 1996, which is ingrained in my memory. I was attending a computing course in a hotel and had a meal of seafood in the evening. I woke in the night feeling absolutely awful. I had sickness, diarrhoea and was shaking all over. There was a seminar at nine o'clock in the morning and in my usual fashion, I made myself presentable and attended. Just like several other unfortunate delegates, I was still sweating and shaking, when we had a mid-morning break. I walked slowly to the car park and slumped into my car feeling quite giddy. I turned on the radio and heard some news that I just did not believe. In my illness I thought I was hallucinating. In Dunblane, Scotland a man had shot dead sixteen small children and a teacher. Crying and shaking in disbelief and sickness, I asked another chap in the car park whether he had heard the news. He had and he confirmed it. I cannot remember anything else that day.

Nonetheless, I am still a happy person, although thoughtful and serious at times too.

-16-

GRANDCHILDREN... or DÉJÀ VU

'Grandchildren are precious gifts given to parents from their children.'
(Lisa, 2005)

'Grandad, was Nanny your first girlfriend?' enquired Emily aged thirteen.

'Well thank you Emily for that question,' I replied. 'You know what it means to learn from your mistakes? Well, I prefer not to make them, because it can be painful. Yes, she was my first proper girlfriend and I got it right first time.' We laughed. Em's a great girl in every way.

I sometimes look upon grandchildren as a most interesting re-run of bringing up our two children. We are fortunate enough to be very hands-on and have seen all the children frequently during their young lives. I cannot help quietly drawing comparisons with our two children, spotting similarities and differences. So far, I am thrilled with the results.

Our son Clive has Emily, born in 1995, and a son Scott, who popped up in 1998. Our daughter Kate has two boys, Jamie born 2005 and Daniel who arrived in 2008. Ruth and I are given unlimited access to them all and they are the sweetest children we could imagine. Lucky old us. They make me feel very happy indeed.

Clive and his wife Victoria divorced in 2004, which was difficult for all concerned, but as amicable as possible. Clive remarried in July 2007 and brings the kids to his new home most weekends. He also speaks to them on the telephone nearly every weekday and he is very proud of them. His wife Debbie is a warm, intelligent young woman, who always makes us welcome and we all get on very well. The children are well supported by all concerned, including Vic's mother Sally, who lives near to us, and are as balanced and happy as most children can be. Vic also made them very proud of their mum, when in July 2009 they saw her awarded a first class honours degree. She then embarked upon a PhD and will surely become the first Dr Brooks.

Emily and Scott enjoy my 'true life stories', which I have had to repeat several times. Many are included in this book, as I thought other children and adults might like them too. Their favourites concern my school pal known as Monkey, but they also like tales of the 'olden days' and any stories where things went wrong. We have watched them go through the sports, hobbies and clubs that many young children try their hands at. Whilst at primary school they both enjoyed sailing and became quite proficient. I thought they were very brave, when they had to deliberately capsize their boats, fall in the cold water of the lake, turn the boats upright again and climb back in! Not for me. Currently, in 2009, they have their academic work at the grammar school as a priority, but Scott is also playing the saxophone and Em has gained a black belt in karate. They are both very high achievers at school and we all know how important education is, if you want a good job eventually, which they say they do. Just before Em left primary school, she was part of the sports team that competed against twenty-five other schools in ten different activities. Her wins in the table tennis (just like her dad) helped clinch the overall victory for her school. Back to the saxophone, as part of Ruth's sixtieth birthday celebrations in 2008, we had a family meal, where Scott surprised his nan by arriving at the restaurant early and playing her into the restaurant with 'Happy birthday to you'.

Once a year, Ruth and I take Emily and Scott on holiday abroad. This has included Denmark, Holland twice and Berlin, but the grandest was three weeks in the USA in 2006. When we took a helicopter flight through the Grand Canyon, I experienced one of those touching moments that really hit home. The four of us shared the cockpit with a young American couple and the pilot. The young chap was fairly quiet at first. When we landed in the canyon for champagne and nibbles, he came over to chat to me.

'They are great kids,' he said. 'Are they your grandchildren?'

'Yes, thanks,' I replied proudly.

'They are very comfortable with you,' he added. 'That's a blessing.'

It seemed such a kind observation to express so openly, for a quiet man, and it made me feel good.

I must say that there was a warm feeling of déjà vu as we flew through the canyon. We had done the same thing twenty-four years earlier with Clive and Kate, which we remember so clearly and fondly.

In July 2010 we will take Em and Scott to Australia and New Zealand via Singapore going out and Hong Kong on the return journey. They will be fourteen and twelve years old by then, so I hope that they can keep up with us!

Grandchildren seem to amuse themselves by associating grey hair and wearing glasses with old age and making sure that their grandparents acknowledge this too. Now, I gave in to greying hair at the age of twenty-one, when I got married, so there may be a connection. Most fortunately, despite years of study, I still do not need glasses. However, when I was fifty, I realised that my hearing was deteriorating. I had tests to prove this, but despite seeing a Harley Street specialist, there seemed to be no obvious reason for it, like family history or being exposed to loud noises. Ruth and I had the quite common problem associated with deafness of me wanting the television louder than she did. I also needed to hear better for my job. Anyway, I opted for a hearing aid rather than an operation. When I was in the company's rather large boardroom, I had found it somewhat embarrassing not knowing what was being said, even with my hand cupped around my ear. Whilst running training courses for a big group, I would walk up to each person that spoke to me; otherwise I just would not have heard them. The hearing aids have been a great success and they fit so well that I can go out running with them in position.

Ruth is rarely fazed by anything, including the deterioration of her eyesight. It had been excellent until she became a grandmother, she says. She realised what was happening, as many people do, when she started holding reading material at arms length in order to focus. She soon gave way to glasses.

So we are 'hear no evil' and 'see no evil'. We try our best to speak no evil, especially in front of the growing family.

I have made a few commitments to the grandchildren. The first is that I will always give them my time, for as long as I am physically able and they want me. So far, so good with that one. We take over Kate's little boys up in Hertfordshire once a fortnight, while she gets on with those things that you cannot do with them around. We also babysit, when we can, and when Ruth retired on 9th July 2009, we were able to be there even more often.

It's over an hour via the dreaded M25, but who cares. It's worth it. We see Clive's two, Em and Scott, several times a week, often collecting them from school. I take Em to and from karate, for which she is now adding to her black belt. In the good weather Scott and I go for a bike ride or ramble once a week, although his homework comes first. The conversations just get better and better. Those two kids are clever and funny. What a great combination. I feel quite sure that being with Jamie and Daniel, as they get older, will be equally rewarding and I already love them and their little characters immensely. I am also glad that they are individuals and little Daniel is not simply a clone of Jamie, great though he is.

The second commitment is to buy each grandchild a car, which will be staggered over about thirteen years, fortunately. The promise was initially made to Emily so that she could drive safely to university one day. That car is getting closer, as she is fourteen as I write this and her dad is giving her some driving instruction, which he had at a similar age.

The third commitment concerns running marathons in their honour. When Em was born, I ran a London Marathon dedicated to her and gave her the medal, suitably inscribed. When Scott came along, I ran the New York and had that medal similarly engraved. Jamie has a Boston medal and baby Daniel has the 2008 Paris version. I also did the Edinburgh in 2008, but ran out of grandchildren. If any more come along, then I will do another twenty-six miler. Otherwise, I will not bother, but it would not be a problem, as I think I could always churn out an occasional marathon.

I must admit that being called 'grandad' did not feel very flattering at first, especially aged forty-eight. However, it has proven to be so much better than not being a grandad. I look forward to being welcomed into their lives by great-grandchildren one day.

Ruth and I on our wedding day - 28th September 1968

Above: Ruth and I at the Statue of Liberty in 1982;
Below: At the top of the Eiffel Tower in 2000

With my children Kate and Clive on their wedding days

From the top, left to right: Grandchildren Emily, Scott, Jamie and Daniel

-17-

MEETING JIMMY GREAVES!

'I have never met a man so ignorant that
I couldn't learn something from him.'
(Galileo, 1600)

'Happy sixtieth birthday, Dad, I've got you and Mum two tickets to 'An Evening with Jimmy Greaves' and Mum said you were free on that date.' My son Clive is both thoughtful and generous with presents.

'Hello Dad, me again. I have just had a call from the Hazlitt Theatre, Maidstone, to say that I was first to book tickets on-line for Jimmy Greaves and that I could meet Jimmy before the show and receive a signed football. I said it would be my dad who would do that. Is that OK?'

OK? Fantastic. I saw Jimmy's debut for Spurs in 1961 and he has always been my favourite player. The meeting with Jimmy, his mate Chopper Harris and Jimmy's event manager was great and to my surprise lasted at least ten minutes with photos. A local newspaper reporter recorded it all in a good spread with a photo of Jimmy and me smiling. Ruth took some smashing pictures of me and Jim, one of which she also made into a mouse mat, so I am looking at it now. Jim's a natural, friendly guy and later gave a terrific stand-up comedy performance. I had never heard any of his jokes and anecdotes before. His manager was a really pleasant chap, who also looked after Pele's UK appearances. I took the opportunity to ask him who Pele thought was the greatest goal-scorer of all time and the answer was Jimmy.

There was an amusing incident in 1962 when England played Brazil and a stray dog ran on the pitch. Various people unsuccessfully chased the animal, but Jimmy knelt down on all fours and beckoned it to come to him. He was able to pick it up, but must have seen the funny side when it peed all over his shirt. The Brazilians were so entertained that one of their players took the dog home as a family pet!

Although he no longer drinks, it is well documented that Jimmy was an alcoholic, which is a great shame for such a nice, intelligent guy. I hope that he is very happy. I know he has at least ten grandchildren and one great-grandchild, so that must please him enormously. Other highly skilled footballers, like George Best and Paul (Gazza) Gascoigne, have had major problems too, sadly declining into alcoholism and despair. I wish we could somehow take more care of our heroes. Good luck in your efforts to turn your life around Gazza.

Apart from Jimmy, Lady Douglas Home, Ricky Gervais (briefly) and Princess Marina (very briefly) I have met quite a number of other famous people, chiefly through work or sporting functions. It makes me wonder with whom I would really like to have had a one-to-one and discover what makes them tick. I am fascinated by those folk from fairly ordinary roots who go on to achieve greatness or excellence. Authors like George Eliot, Charles Dickens and the Brontes would be on my literary list, as I cannot believe the fantastic use of beautiful words that they achieved. Books like Middlemarch by Eliot and Tale of Two Cities by Dickens just astound me. Winston Churchill would be on my historical list, mostly for his decision-making. Ruth and I visited the Orkney Islands in Scotland in 2004 and saw the naval defence barriers he had built in the 1940s to protect the Royal Navy anchorage at Scapa Flow. It was one example of the decisive actions he took to protect his country. I remember his death in January 1965 and have visited his home at Chartwell in Kent on several enjoyable occasions. He did not get everything right in his career, but he was a great man and I thank him.

Having been a minor shareholder in Tottenham Hotspur, I eventually attended my first AGM in December 2008. It was excellent. Our recently appointed manager and saviour, Harry Redknapp, was unveiled, as were the plans for a new stadium. The evening concluded with a question and answer session, which was long, frank and wide-ranging. Then, to my surprise, the board, including the chairman Daniel Levy, stayed around to chat to individuals. I was pleased to shake the hands of several board members, including Daniel, and ask them various questions, which they answered in a friendly, earnest manner. I was very pleased as I drove home to Kent from Tottenham that evening, despite the usual dreadful traffic in the Blackwall Tunnel.

During 2009, Tottenham Hotspur Football Club backed the production of a book written entirely by fans, so I sent in my article and photograph. Fortunately, it was chosen and I was invited to the book launch in their stadium, White Hart Lane. I took my son Clive and it was a great evening, sharing memories and meeting Spurs 'legends' like Les Ferdinand, Clive Allen, Pat Jennings and the Welsh Wizard from the 'double' side Cliff Jones. Clive and I got autographs, handshakes, photographs and conversations with them all and what a really nice bunch of chaps they are. The two Clives, Brooks and Allen, were engrossed in a discussion about one of Mr Allen's goals from the 1980s that he hit incredibly hard with almost no backlift. I spent more time with Cliff, who played with Clive's dad, Les Allen, and Jimmy Greaves when they won the league and cup double. What a perfect evening for Clive and I to drive home chatting about Spurs. Now, as a bit of serendipity, I shortly received an email from another contributor to the book who shared my surname. He had read my article, which included my dad and grandad being Spurs supporters from Bethnal Green. My family history seemed to match his so closely that we spoke on the telephone and met at his home. So, I now have a previously unknown, distant cousin David Brooks, who not only followed the right path to Spurs, but like my son and I, believes Glenn Hoddle to be the most skilful footballer of all time, bar none.

Whilst on the subject of Spurs, which I am quite often, I was surprised many years ago to find myself queuing to enter the ground behind that great comedian Peter Cook. Apparently he was Spurs through and through, not using his fame or money for a special seat, but queuing to stand and watch like the rest of us. Although I did not meet him, in recent years I saw the former leader of the Conservative Party, Iain Duncan Smith sitting in the crowd. I think it is interesting that so many people from all walks of life take great pleasure in watching football.

While I was in the business world, I did accept some hospitality at Spurs, meeting great players and managers like Glenn Hoddle. I once spent quite some time talking to Warren Mitchell, who was nothing like his television character Alf Garnett! Anyway, Alf supported West Ham and Warren is a lifelong Spurs fan.

I often saw, to my pleasure, Charles Hodges and David Peacock, otherwise known as Chas and Dave. They sometimes performed several of their hits on the pitch as pre-match entertainment. Even Chas and Dave's records about Spurs did quite well in the charts with 'Ossie's Dream' reaching number five. I must say that I have to agree with the duo's insistence, 'Give me a London girl every time'.

One evening, after a Spurs game, Clive rang BBC Radio Five Live's 606 football phone-in to speak to the presenter, Tory MP David Mellor, who knows his 'footy'. Clive was chosen to speak to David on air, which usually lasts a minute or two. David is a Chelsea fan and the two of them were absolutely engrossed in conversation. After around twenty minutes, David said, 'Well, Clive, it's been good chatting to you, but I had better say goodbye and move on.' Actually, the conversation nearly failed to take place, as my phone was plugged into the cigarette lighter and it cut out when I switched off the engine in order to hear them talk! However, we were reconnected and it all went very well.

My son is a fan of the band Oasis and met Noel Gallagher (another man who knows his footy) at the bar during a break in a concert. Clive shook his hand and thanked him for the great music. Clive described him as a nice chap who acted as though he had never been asked to shake someone's hand before, but was pleased by the act.

Returning to sport, Ruth and I went to the Wimbledon Lawn Tennis tournament (or grand slam) twice via their Public Ticket Lottery. We were extremely lucky in 2004 to get tickets for Centre Court on ladies final day, Saturday 3rd July. As soon as we entered the grounds, we stood right next to an outside court while the all-conquering Martina Navratilova warmed up and joked with us in the small crowd. Once inside Centre Court, we took our superb seats close to the net and saw the fantastic Roger Federer complete a semi-final win, held over from the previous rain-spoilt day. The twenty-two year old Swiss beat Sebastien Grosjean of France in straight sets and we were most fortunate to see probably the greatest male player of all time, thanks to Friday's rain. The ladies final was absolutely staggering. A pretty, blonde, very young looking seventeen year old Russian named Maria Sharapova put on a stunning display of power and poise to beat the hot favourite Serena Williams 6-1, 6-4. Most people remember her on the telephone to her mother, I believe, and climbing up through the crowd to hug her family, but during the presentation ceremony, I was glued to the Williams family. As Maria received her prize, Serena was all smiles for the youngster and Serena's mother applauded warmly for her daughter's winning opponent. Talk about gracious in defeat. It was an exceptional occasion, which we shared with the nearby Margaret Thatcher, John

McEnroe, Virginia Wade and Ann Jones. Now there is a sportswoman, because when she was Ann Haydon, she was in the table tennis world championship finals for singles, doubles and mixed doubles in 1957 and, on getting married, she became Wimbledon Lawn Tennis champion in 1969. In 2005, Ruth and I got seats for the second Monday at Wimbledon, so it was not as exciting as the previous year. However, it was Number One Court and we saw Sharapova win again, a straight sets victory by America's Andy Roddick and the French player Amelie Mauresmo going through comfortably into the next round.

Other famous people that I encountered? Well, whilst at university, around 1966, I met Sir Fred Hoyle, the most eminent astronomer. He was a brilliant man, in great demand for lecturing to budding scientists on both sides of the Atlantic, but he will probably be remembered chiefly for his rejection of the Big Bang theory. However, I will always be able to visualise the scene when he gave us a presentation, as he made quite a gaffe. Perhaps geniuses do that sort of thing. He was illustrating his speech by projecting images onto the white square of a moving 'blackboard', just like we had at school years ago. He was not a tall man and used a stick to point to items on the screen. As his stick was not quite long enough to touch the area he was telling us about, he pulled down the board. There was a gasp in the audience, as the projected image obviously did not move down, but the board did. He quickly pushed the white square back up and carried on successfully. Just a little blip, but it seemed odd for a great scientist.

In the early 1990s, I attended a 'jolly' with others in the IT world. It was a day of fun and competitive driving experiences at Bruntingthorpe in Leicestershire. The venue was constructed in 1942 as a World War II airfield and used by the US Air Force, but later became a vehicle test track facility and hosted corporate events. One of the activities was to drive a small racing car around a track in the fastest time within a group of six guests. The cars had Cosworth engines, as used in Formula One, so could go pretty fast. We were each taken in a two-seater by a professional driver for a demonstration circuit, before having five attempts on our own. My man happened to be former racing driver and BBC commentator Dr Jonathan Palmer. He had previously participated in 87 Formula One grand prix, so I paid attention. He took it easy, but set a good time for us to aim at. After my first solo lap, I had achieved a reasonable time and was lying second out of six contestants, largely due to four of them going too fast and spinning off! After each successive lap, I had managed to lower my time, but dropped a place as another chap did a fast time. One by one the other guys were calming down a bit and avoiding spins, but striving hard to pick up seconds on the straights. I just wanted each of my laps to be better than the previous one, but after the five attempts I was a slightly disappointing sixth. I realised that it was in my nature to try to improve steadily without making mistakes, whereas, because it was just a bit of competitive fun, the other guys were really going for it. Some had only one or two good, fast laps and several disastrous ones. Thinking about it afterwards, I would have liked another five or ten laps to see whether my approach would progressively knock more seconds off my time and move me up towards the top. Interesting. As usual, it made me think about the way I approach things. However, the evening meal was great fun and Dr Palmer gave a really absorbing after-dinner speech.

In 1998, whilst leading a company culture change project about teamworking, we had a rather grand corporate event, chaired by our American chief executive. The highlight was the surprise appearance of the British athlete Kriss Akabusi, who had turned his talents to motivational speaking. In order to help demonstrate teamwork, he showed a video of the 4 x 400 meters relay race in the World Championships in Tokyo in 1991. It was in this event that Great Britain with Kriss on the last leg beat the USA, who were hot favourites. The four Americans were all individually faster than the four Britons and Kriss, a hurdler, overtook the current world champion to win the gold medal in one of the most exciting races I had ever seen. Our chief executive made a strong but humble speech about British teamwork overcoming American individuality and what lessons we could learn. This was fine, but the bonus was that I managed to get ten minutes of Kriss's time just for myself to talk not about teamwork, but running. He was great to listen to and I did feel inspired by his words and sheer enthusiasm.

I have for many years belonged to an historical society and met some very interesting characters. In 1999 we were in London with the writer Lucinda Lambton, with whom we shared a bottle of wine. She often appeared on television and had written a book on the history of the lavatory, which was not my favourite subject, but she was very chatty and most amusing in our company. I seem to remember that she left our group to meet her husband Sir Peregrine Worsthorne, another author and broadcaster. Soon after that we had tea with Princess Olga Romanoff at her home in Kent. She is descended from the Russian House of Romanov and is a cousin of HRH Queen Elizabeth II, so we had a very interesting chat in her kitchen.

Just a few years ago, I worked in the same department as the brother of a future British prime minister. My colleague was not famous then, but he hit the headlines today (8th May 2009) when he allegedly shared a large cleaning bill with his sibling, which appeared at first to be at the taxpayer's expense. I am being a bit mysterious, I know.

Oh, I almost forgot Jamie Oliver. I bumped into him in the restaurant of a hotel in Cologne, when he was doing some work for German television. He was in a friendly little group and they invited us to join them, but my companions were reticent and I had to politely decline. Pity, as he seems to be a genuine guy, so it would have been nice to have had a longer conversation.

Now, here's a more tenuous tale (a little alliteration) regarding meeting people. It concerns my great-grandmother, Louisa Dyer, bumping into a certain mysterious person. She lived in the parish of Whitechapel, east London, and was on her way home one dark winter's evening. The year was 1888. She was thirty-three years old, very poor and married with nine children. Unlike many women in her neighbourhood, she had not been driven to prostitution. She told the following story to her daughter Edith, who told my mother Lilian. A tall, sinister gentleman, wearing a black top hat and long black coat stopped her in an alley. There was another man with him nearby. The tall man asked her a few questions, then he said, 'You are obviously a good girl' and let her hurry away. She felt sure that it was Jack the Ripper. So, there's a fair chance that one of my ancestors met somebody famous, or infamous. Incidentally, Louise and her labourer husband William went on to produce seventeen children. It could be said that contraception was non-existent among the poor around that time, but at least she survived the possible 'Ripper' and died of old age.

Meeting people for the first time, whether famous or not, interests me and is usually a pleasure, as I am probably in their company due to a mutual concern, like music or sport. I was recently chatting to some Conservative Party agents, who I met by chance, and we discussed the merits of politicians like David Cameron, William Hague and Margaret Thatcher, all of whom they encountered quite frequently. I do enjoy getting the 'inside track' on people in the public eye that have been or may at some stage be relevant to me and my family's future happiness.

-18-

OF ROYAL DESCENT

'Mighty oaks from little acorns grow'
(Geoffrey Chaucer, 1374)

'Larry, it's Sandra, are you sitting down? I've found Lionel Williams Moyle Dyer.' That was in March 2005 and Sandra was a friend doing some family history research for me in Devon. I had started building my family tree in 1976 and Sandra had found the missing link.

Way back in the seventies, my brother asked, 'Larry, do you think we're Jewish? Mum thinks we may be Scottish, but her family lived in east London and look Jewish.' I replied, 'Gordon, I don't know, so I'll find out. Ruth has some of her family tree mapped out on a piece of wallpaper, so I will trace our ancestry and sketch that out too. Hopefully, we'll finally know the truth.' I also decided at that time that I would combine our trees and collect photographs of everyone, where possible, with our own children at the bottom of the chart.

It is said that most of us are descended from King Edward III, but that was not of interest to me when I started. I did everything the hard way, as nothing was computerised until the Mormons put their huge database on an accessible medium. Having spoken to relatives and obtained as much information as possible, I started to compile our family tree. I dredged for information from county record offices, churches and all other well-known sources. By the early 1980s I had a comprehensive tree going back over two hundred years on both sides of our families, including Ruth's forebears

Robert and Elizabeth Browning. No, not those two, but a gas fitter and a midwife, who were as equally useful as their famous namesakes. By 1985 I had twenty-three individual photographs of our ancestors. I have since added to that another ten photos of us and our descendants. I still have my photographic family tree, with our four grandchildren at the bottom.

I have also visited church graveyards and cemeteries, searching which can be something of a hit and miss activity. I once took Kate with me to look for family gravestones in Abney Park Cemetery in north-east London. Just like the famous Highgate Cemetery, it was built around 1840 to cope with London's rapid increase in population and deaths. It is both a cemetery and a vast public park, right on Stoke Newington High Street. It is probably the best example of natural woodland in the London area. Unfortunately, it was closed by the police on the day of our visit. A constable informed me that a body had been found in the cemetery!

Tracing our history reunited me with my cousin David, a really nice chap whom I had not seen since we were small boys and there we were in our forties. He had an engineering degree from Cambridge and his hobby was photography. While we discussed the family tree and exchanged old photographs, I showed him a picture I had just taken of a quaint little cottage in Abbots Langley, Hertfordshire, where our great-grandmother had been born in 1863. Most surprisingly, David took one look and showed me photographs he had taken of the same area. He had been the civil engineer responsible for building the stretch of the M25 that now ran right beside the cottage. I do like serendipity.

Over the years, I managed to go back a bit further with my research and found a few more names here and there, but there was always a particular puzzle on my mother's side.

For many generations, our ancestors were from London with a little immigration from Hertfordshire, Norfolk and Devon. People usually made this move from the rural areas to find work in the big towns. These past family members were all, it seems, straight-forward, Church of England, working folk, with which I am very comfortable.

My mother's mother was one of seventeen children, nine of whom died in poverty in east London, but Mum's sister and brother both thought we had a knight of the realm in our ancestry. They referred to him as Sir Lionel Fairclough Dyer, but it was all by word of mouth. I found that their great-grandfather was a schoolmaster, Lionel William Dyer, according to his marriage certificate. Thanks to my research on the Internet, I met a previously unknown second cousin of mine named Mike, who is also descended from Lionel. His mother Eve was orphaned at a very young age and we managed to arrange for her to meet my mum, who was her first cousin. Eve was thrilled and it was all rather emotional. Strangely, using the on-line Mormon record, I also found a Lionel Moyle Dyer, but he appeared to be six years older than my Lionel and was from Devon, as well as having a different middle name. I eventually discovered that my Lionel was also originally from Devon. To cut a very long story short, my friend Sandra had found that it was one person, Lionel Williams Moyle Dyer, my great-great-grandfather.

This is where the fun began. I easily found Lionel's father to be one Foscarinus Turtliff Dyer and, no, I do not know where that first name came from, despite my efforts. Turtliff was his mother's maiden name, which seems to have died out as a surname.

Foscarinus, who was born in 1755, became a freeman of Plymouth and chief clerk in the naval dockyard. His father was Robert Dyer, a shopkeeper and ship's purser, who died in the Falkland Islands in 1769. It took over a year for the news of his death to reach his widow Sarah, as there was no internet, email or telephone! Sarah had to apply to the Navy for a pension, which was initially denied because they had been informed more than a year after his death. However, I read the original historic papers in the National Archives at Kew confirming that she got the pension on appeal. In addition, I took a copy of his fine copperplate handwriting in the ship's log, which stopped, of course, the day he died. There is also a memorial to Robert near Port Egmont on Saunders Island, where the British first settled in the Falklands in 1765. In 2007, a lady on that island kindly photographed it with a digital camera and emailed it to me in less than two hours from my request. How communications have improved. As I mentioned earlier, Ruth and I visited the Falklands in December 2009 and saw where my ancestor was buried. It wasn't all about family history, as the penguins and albatrosses were amazing. We had a really interesting and exciting time, especially as we went via Rio de Janeiro and the breathtaking Iguassu Falls in Brazil!

I have read a great deal about the chequered history of the Falkland Islands around the time of Robert's voyage. Apparently, in 1770, the year after Robert died, his ship HMS Favourite was forced to surrender to four Spanish vessels after defending the settlement against these invaders. I know it was also protecting other ships, but I would love to know exactly what the Favourite was embarked upon and why Robert died, but so far I have had no luck finding this out. I will keep trying, as it is important to help understand why the Falklands truly belongs to Britain.

Robert's father-in-law, Richard Boger, was interestingly described in 1749 as both a surgeon for the Royal Navy and an apothecary, which I think of as a pharmacist. Foscarinus' father-in-law was William Stephens, who was variously listed around 1740 as a doctor or surgeon in the Royal Navy, an apothecary and 'an oculist of some fame'. I did find letters that he had exchanged with another leading British eye specialist, so it seems that he did some important work in that field.

In 2005 I went to the grand Norman church of St Germans in Cornwall, where Robert had been a churchwarden, and found memorials to Robert's ancestors and other relatives. He was in fact the illegitimate son of Walter Moyle (hence my g-g-grandfather's middle name) and one Micah Dyer. Walter died aged twenty-two having just matriculated at Oxford University. Walter's brother John, Sheriff of Cornwall, left £400 to Robert in his will, which was a considerable sum in 1748. Walter and John were the sons of Sir Walter Moyle, also Sheriff of Cornwall, whose ancestry was easy to trace back to King Edward III, as all this is well documented. Hence my twenty-five times great grandfather is William the Conqueror.

This does mean that my family tree includes Ethelred the Unready, Alfred the Great and royalty from all over Europe and Scandinavia. All of this is quite interesting, but highly irrelevant really, because my life was only significantly influenced by one level of my ancestry, Mum and Dad.

However, it may explain why the Queen and Prince Philip waved to me one day. They somehow knew I was a cousin. I was driving home from work, when the traffic was stopped by a police car on a local roundabout. I got out of the car to stretch my legs, when a police outrider drove past me followed by a rather grand car containing their royal highnesses. I waved to them and they waved back majestically. As I was standing on my own, it must have been personal. After all, Prince Philip of Greece chose my actual birthday, 18th March 1947, to become a naturalised Briton and in November that year, as Lieutenant Philip Mountbatten, he married HRH Princess Elizabeth.

Just like many others who trace their ancestry, I get completely engrossed in the research and have had a great deal of enjoyment from it. All in all, I do find it stabilising and satisfying to know my roots.

-19-

AIN'T NATURE WONDERFUL

'Make the boy interested in natural history if you can'
(Robert Falcon Scott, March 1912)

'Make the boy interested in natural history if you can'. What a surprising entry to make in the last letter you will ever write to your wife, whilst waiting for your death. Robert Falcon Scott was a British Royal Naval officer famous for his second and final expedition to the Antarctic region. He and his companions were to reach the South Pole, but die of hunger, exhaustion and cold. He became a national hero, dubbed Scott of the Antarctic. The boy he mentions was his son Peter, then aged just two and a half. Scott's wife must have responded to that advice about the boy, as he went on to become Sir Peter Scott, one of the greatest naturalists of all time.

I have a small coincidence with Peter Scott, who, unlike me, was an accomplished artist. I had art lessons at school and the only painting that I can remember producing was of his father, Robert. I was aged eleven and I painted a scene where Scott and his companions were trudging through snow in a blizzard. I do not think that the picture was well executed, but my art teacher liked the way that I had snow swirling around their faces and bodies. He chose it among a small group to represent our school's efforts at an exhibition in Edmonton Town Hall, north London, so I was very proud of that.

I have mentioned previously my lifelong interest in birds, but my love of nature really covers the length and breadth of British flora and fauna. As an example, being an odd little lad, I would find different varieties of ladybirds in my garden and cross-breed them in containers. I provided them with greenfly to eat and plants on which to lay their eggs and soon the larvae would hatch. I nurtured these until they pupated and I managed to produce some ladybirds with new patterns on their little wing cases. I once found about a dozen different ladybirds in my garden, out of more than fifty potential varieties. You will be lucky to find one now, apart from the harlequin, which started appearing in Britain in 2004 and is now very well established indeed.

Just like my dad, I became interested in genetics. I had always looked upon the inbreeding of birds and animals as a bad thing, likely to produce offspring with problems. That was until I went to see the wild white cattle at Chillingham in Northumberland. They are said to be survivors of the wild herds that once roamed our forests and this herd was enclosed in parkland in the 13th century. Scientists are fascinated as to how they have been inbred for so long without any significant problems. I believe that the size of the herd has varied from as high as eighty to a low of thirteen in the unusually hard winter of 1946-1947, when, as it happens I was born. Only one mature bull survived at that time, so the inbreeding was total and the animals genetically pure. Most people with herds of cattle or deer try to ensure that a new male takes over the role of servicing the females every year or two in order to avoid incest, but the Chillingham Wild Cattle just go on and on.

I had also read about an experiment with guppies, the small tropical fish. A tank of guppies had been kept for many years without the introduction of fresh blood. The longest that a guppy is likely to live is about two years, if it is lucky, so there had been much incest going on to keep the community thriving. However, little or no defects occurred in the fish. Trying the same experiment, I have also had tanks of guppies for many years with no newcomers and numbers sometimes dropping quite low, but on they go, totally inbred.

In 1995, I decided to erect a dovecote in my garden and all I needed was some white doves. I was offered a pair, but wondered how they would decide to use my cote and not just disappear. The expert told me to keep them in a small cage attached to one nesting hole in the cote until they laid their traditional two eggs in the hole. When you remove the cage, they will fly free, but return to incubate their eggs and rear their young. What is more, they would produce offspring every eight weeks or so. My next question was about attracting mates for these offspring, but the answer was that this was unnecessary, as the siblings would breed with one another and inhabit the other nesting holes! This is indeed what happened. My initial pair, Saffy and Waffy, if you remember the protocol, became great, great, great grandparents. When Waffy died, Saffy took up with one of his great granddaughters and lived happily ever after.

I still enjoy bird-watching, as does Ruth. It takes us to some beautiful places, where in addition to our feathered friends, we discover various wild animals and plants. For example, we frequently visit our local RSPB reserve at Elmley in Kent. With little effort we see between thirty and fifty different species of birds each time we go, including marsh harriers, owls and avocets. As I write this, at the end of May 2009, baby avocets are in abundance. They are like balls of fluff on little sticks. In the last two years at Elmley we have also seen baby bunnies, hares boxing, a family of stoats cavorting around the edges of the marsh, water voles and giant green marsh frogs. Not a bad haul.

I have never been a twitcher. These folk seem to live in order to see a new bird, travelling as far as it takes to join all the others obsessed in that way. The poor bird is often a stray, arriving at that destination by chance or strong winds. Sometimes these rarities have simply escaped from captivity, like a wildlife park or zoo. I simply want to see our lovely British birds, even if I cannot specifically identify them all. What does it matter? Just enjoy. However, let me tell you about some fairly rare and unusual birds I have seen that many birders would appreciate. Among the raptors or birds of prey that we aspire to spot are, of course, golden eagles and osprey. The former are straightforward to see, if you go to the right places in Scotland, like the Isle of Mull. I first went looking for osprey in 1976 at the famous RSPB site in Loch Garten, also in Scotland. It was out of season, but we were there anyway with our two children, who were very young. We stood under the tree that was the regular nesting site chatting to a German ornithologist and bemoaning the lack of ospreys. Suddenly little Kate cried out for some reason and a splendid osprey took off majestically above us, gliding around for a while. Somehow, I was more thrilled for the German chap, as he had come a long way to see the birds and we had not let him down. I have since had some marvellous views of osprey nesting and catching fish, thanks to having our very good friends Dave and Jean living in Scotland.

As most people probably know, cuckoos are interesting birds, famous for laying their eggs in the nests of smaller birds. These unfortunate parents kindly rear the baby cuckoo, who repays them by murdering their babies. He pushes the eggs or chicks out of the nest so that he can get all the food. He becomes so large that his foster parents often stand on his back to feed him. I had occasionally heard the distinctive cry of a cuckoo and once seen the bird fly quickly by, until in 1972 I attended a local course in bird-watching. We were not looking for cuckoos, but saw three of them jumping around playfully on a fence. I call this odd, because they lay one egg in each nest and are not exactly family-oriented. Years later I was telling Dave and Jean about this as we strolled around an idyllic loch near their home in Scotland, when suddenly three cuckoos appeared just ahead of us. Too many spooky coincidences have occurred in my life over the decades, so I was surprised but not worried by yet another one. Incidentally, I like links and coincidences, so I must mention that Dave and Jean spent their first date watching Spurs at White Hart Lane, just like us. Their two sons are Paul, my godson, who sensibly supports Spurs, and Ian who follows, guess who, Manchester United. Great lads who with their wives Georgina and Lynn always warmly welcome us to Bonnie Scotland.

All birders would like to see a bittern, as they are so rare. They sneak around the edges of marshes and until 2006 I had not spotted one. Ruth and I had become interested in the new wetlands that were being developed around Britain and were visiting them all over a period of time. We were in Wales for non-birding reasons and to our surprise came across a sign for a wetland near Cardiff, so we took a look. It was a bit late in the afternoon and most birders were leaving, but we walked out to a hide, where there was one chap with his eye glued to his telescope. I heard him say 'bittern' without moving a muscle. He dare not lose sight of such a rare find, but quickly described to me where it was. I was able to watch the bird until it was time for us to go. Back at the entrance to the wetland I told some birders, who were just leaving, that I had seen a bittern and they all leapt into action, grabbed their gear and ran off to the hide. I hope they had some luck. In November 2009 we saw our second bittern, but this was planned. We went on a 'bittern safari' with the RSPB at Dungeness in Kent and one generously flew right in front of us!

Another unusual occurrence was a sighting of waxwings, which are rather splendid visitors to Britain. We heard that three had been spotted locally in Gillingham and twitchers with telescopes appeared from everywhere. I popped over and saw one bird myself. However, whilst my student daughter Kate was living in a crummy little flat on a crowded concrete estate in Hatfield, Hertfordshire, she enquired of me, on one of my visits, 'What are those birds on that bush Dad?' 'There are about twenty-five waxwings' I replied. 'That's pretty unusual. They must somehow know about that little bush covered in berries tucked away next to your flat'. Amazing.

Lastly, nuthatches. A perky little blue and chestnut bird that scurries around trees looking for insects. I had only seen two in my life, one of which came to my garden. They are not really rare, but you feel lucky to spot one. Well, a few years ago, Ruth and I were sitting in our Ford Cortina in a car park at Tarr Steps, Exmoor in Somerset. We were eating sandwiches, when five cheeky nuthatches (no, not colourful sparrows) landed on the bonnet and wing mirror, begging for food. This kind of thing makes birdwatching quite a fascinating pastime.

To be honest, I mostly combine our visits to reserves and wetlands with our desire to travel, but I do love nature and it adds much to our general feeling of wellbeing and happiness.

Much of our pleasure with nature comes from our own back garden, which is modest in size, but a haven for wildlife. We have seen fifty species of bird in the garden, including non-natives like green parakeets, plus foxes, hedgehogs, squirrels and bats. There are plenty of bushes and wild areas for them to hide in or nest. They all enjoy a drink from our pond, where we have frogs, newts and goldfish too. We feed the birds all year round and make sure that their favourite shelled sunflower seeds, known as hearts, are always available.

Unfortunately, we have occasionally had birds fly into our windows, which they failed to see, so I have placed stickers on the relevant panes and that dangerous activity has stopped. Before I took that action, I picked up a little feathered body from our extension roof and was surprised not to recognise the species. I held it in my palm and compared it with pictures in my numerous bird books until we decided that it was a garden warbler. We were pleased that it was a 'first' for our garden, but sad at its demise. That was until it awoke and shot off like a rocket! It was only stunned, like the Norwegian Blue parrot in Monty Python.

Many people have seen badgers, which I used to consider to be quite rare. Back in 1973, we were very keen to see one, so we decided that we must try very hard to achieve this. As I mentioned previously, we had a farmhouse holiday in Northumberland, when Clive was one year old and Ruth just pregnant with Kate. It was the day before we got the news that my father-in-law had died that we were chatting to the farmer about badgers. He told us how we could definitely see one. It involved him and his wife babysitting, while Ruth and I took a certain route to a bush in a field, staying down-wind and keeping quiet until the badger appeared at about eight o'clock. We followed his instructions and were hiding behind the bush, when brock turned up right on cue. It was quite thrilling to see our big black and white friend snuffling around, but I think I was more impressed by the plan actually working. Thirty-six years later, I am less impressed with badgers, as they keep tearing up my son's lawn, which I laid!

One morning a few years ago, I was not too pleased with nature, when, ready for work, I popped into the garden for a quick look around. I felt something touch the top of my head, so I brushed my hair with my hand. I immediately suffered a sharp pain beside my thumb. A huge hornet had stung me. I managed to fling it away, but I was soon aware of a swelling in my hand. Luckily, I was able to remove the ring from my finger, before it got too big. I drove to work, as I never miss that joy, but by mid-morning the hand was huge. It had no visible creases and looked like a horrific, inflated rubber glove. I tried to keep it hidden and warned colleagues, especially my PA, not to look at it, because it was pretty hideous. She insisted on seeing it and actually shrieked in horror. By this stage, even I realised that I should see a doctor. I did pop and see him and I believe he gave me anti histamine, which thankfully returned the hand to normal size. Still on the subject of insect stings, I was aware that there was an allergic reaction to wasp venom known as anaphylactic shock. I also knew that victims might die unless treated immediately via an injection of adrenaline. However, I was not sure whether you made yourself more or less liable to this reaction by your own fear or behaviour. Whilst out running alone in a country lane, I was stung on the lip by a wasp, which I had to pull off and throw away. I decided to ignore it and keep running, as I was only a mile or so from home. By the time I got back, I had actually forgotten it had happened and when I remembered to tell my wife, there was little sign of a mark on my skin. Hopefully, I have the right attitude to wasp stings or at least a way of coping that suits my mind and body. A stranger wasp bite occurred on a picnic, when I picked up an open can of drink and took a mouthful. A wasp that was lurking inside entered my mouth and stung my upper pallet. I did not like the idea of this at all. Again, I had to pluck it from the damaged area and fling it away. A lady in our group saw this incident and miraculously produced a bottle of vinegar, which I swilled around my mouth. The potentially dangerous swelling really had little chance to get under way, when the acidic vinegar did its job of neutralising the alkaline venom. Top tip: take vinegar on picnics.

In the year 2008, we had to have our beloved oak tree removed. It was dying fast, as confirmed by the local council's tree department. The problem was put down to the great storm of 1987 when tons of debris were dumped in our garden, making it impossible to actually enter the area without a borrowed chain saw. Fallen branches were window high across the back of our house. In December 2007, an expert told us that water had probably got into some high, broken branches of the oak and spent years freezing and lifting the bark till it all started to fall off in huge chunks. The tree was about 150 years old, 75 feet high and two men could not join hands around the trunk. I would tackle most things, but not the removal of that tree. This became an interesting lesson in making sure that you get more than one quote for a job, the cost of which you would find it difficult to estimate yourself. Read on. Thanks to Gillingham Council and other parties, I drew up a list of tree surgeons and contacted seven to give me a quote. Two firms came to have a look, puffed their cheeks in dismay and apologized for not being able to tackle a job that size. Fair enough. I eventually got quotes from the other five firms. These ranged – wait for it – from £2,000 to £12,000 for the same job. Mr £12,000 did not inspire me with confidence, fortunately. For a start, when he shook hands with me, I noticed that he had a thumb missing, presumably due to an accident. He also spent twenty minutes standing in silence in my neighbour's garden staring at the tree. All five companies mentioned the option of setting up a crane in the street and lifting the tree over our house and garage. The crane would block our close for a day and only one company said they would put notes through neighbours' doors the day before to explain what was to happen. All in all, I did not like the sound of this method. Due to the cost of hiring the crane, it was the same price to use manual labour to chop up the tree in my rear garden and carry it out to their lorries, so I opted for the latter. The other four quotes ranged from £2,000 to £4,600, but one increased by £2,000, when he had a second look. The big issue was the need for a top-class 'climber'. He is the chap who actually goes up the tree, secures ropes and cuts through the branches and trunk. He needs to be brave, strong and methodical in order to do the job safely for all concerned. The firm I chose charged £2,400 and did a splendid job. So, get at least three quotes for any significant project, if you can. Incidentally, it is nothing to do with nature, but reinforces the point, when I tell you that although we had only two quotes for a new kitchen, one was 50% higher than the other, with identical specification. The less expensive company produced an attractive kitchen, which still works very well many years later. We also had two main quotes for an extension to our house, one of which was exactly double the other. We had seen the previous work of the chap with the lower estimate, gave him the work and he was excellent. It is still standing after more than twenty-five years with no problems.

Some months after the demise of our oak tree, I was delighted when two friends, Phil and Celia, presented us with six hand-crafted wooden bowls that Phil had turned from various different pieces of the tree. We kept four and gave Clive and Kate one each. After all, we all lived with that tree for many years.

Let us leap right past my pre-occupation with British birds, mammals and quotes to my present day activities. In the year 2007 I joined the local Bredhurst Woodland Action Group or BWAG, formed to improve the state of the nearby woods. Initially it was a case of removing many tons of rubbish, including burnt out cars, old tyres and empty cash dispensers or ATMs. Then, with the help of the Army, the team filled in huge muddy holes and laid new paths. There are many groups around Britain working on this kind of project, not just us. We also put up new fencing to enclose certain areas and allow sheep to graze. As we have chalk downs in Kent, our borrowed sheep munched the grass nice and short, which enabled the return of natural plants like primroses and orchids. We also borrowed two nice brown Exmoor ponies that kindly ate some of the scrub and brambles. Another part of the grand plan is coppicing. This is a form of woodland management whereby trees like birch are cut down to almost ground level every fifteen years or so. A small percentage of the woodland is coppiced each year and new shoots will appear around the base of each felled tree. As you progress annually around the wood, this has the effect of providing different heights of coppiced trees and a rich variety of habitats. This is beneficial for biodiversity and species of plants and birds not seen for many years will, hopefully, start returning to the site. So there you have it, a good plan and a great achievement so far, much of which I put down to the determination and leadership of a lady named Vanessa.

In order to increase the knowledge of our group, we have various walks led by experts. This has included looking for birds, butterflies, moths, wild flowers, fungi, bats, reptiles and amphibians. During the reptile walk, I chatted to one of the team leaders about attracting and observing snakes. You can do this by placing pieces of flat metal on the grass. The animals go under them to take the warmth that they need to raise their cold-blooded body temperature. He told me that in order to lure slow worms, which are legless lizards, you should place pieces of roofing felt on the ground. Well, call it coincidence or serendipity, but the very next day I was out for a run and curiosity led me down a path beside the M2 motorway that I had never explored before. I emerged in a sunny pasture and found dozens of squares of felt scattered all over the area. I lifted one and found a note in a polythene bag explaining that it was a wildlife survey and to please replace the material. I also found a slow worm under that square. By the time I had looked under them all there were sixty of these reptiles plus twenty-five lizards. Twenty-four hours earlier I had not even heard about this activity, but now I have some roofing felt squares and slow worms in my own garden.

So, what about the future of nature in this country, I hear you ask. First we need to make these lovely places available to a wide variety of users, not just the owners or carers. If families, dog-walkers, horse-riders, cyclists and all other decent folk want to use these areas, then the justification for these natural beauty spots is even greater. Secondly we need joined-up thinking and joined-up vegetation. By joined-up thinking I mean that all flora and fauna conservation groups must work with one another, as well as with landowners, councils and utilities. This has already been realised and is happening in Kent for example. By joined-up vegetation I mean the actual linking of areas like woodlands, parks and reserves to form continuous corridors for birds and animals to travel widely and populate more areas. Conversely, it has been shown that if you run a simple roadway through a wood, it decimates the number of creatures that it can sustain. We must find ways to provide links from one currently separate natural area to another and start reversing that action considerably. This too is being done across Britain, often with some ingenuity, especially if there is a motorway dividing the spaces. People are rising to the challenge and I am very pleased with what I have seen so far.

One important subject that is getting much-needed publicity is the frightening world-wide shortage of bees to pollinate the plants that contribute to our food supplies. I know a number of individuals trying to do their bit by setting up bee hives, but there needs to be international government action immediately to rectify what is a very serious problem.

As I live less than a mile from farmland and countryside, I know for a fact that many species of British birds are dropping in numbers quite dramatically, like yellowhammers and skylarks. In a special survey, nineteen species of farmland birds are counted each year and despite numbers being up for magpies and woodpigeons, the overall population is down by a half since the 1970's. Three-quarters of the countryside is managed by farmers and many more of them need to devote some of their land to the preservation of our precious wildlife. A number of them are already doing a great job.

So, how will non-nature lovers benefit from positive action on wildlife and the environment? Fresh air to breathe, bees to pollinate our food supply and the appreciation of sheer beauty – the thing that separates us from animals. I am not really qualified to lecture on sustainability and the environment, but that won't stop me.

In August 2009, I was speaking to a young chap from Sweden about life in his country. Although there is natural beauty, in his view it is not always available to enjoy due to weather conditions. In winter there are dark days as well as dark nights and in northern Sweden winter lasts for seven months. This causes significant depression in the population and helps lead to a relatively high suicide rate. He referred to this as the seasonal affective disorder (SAD) and concluded that if you live in a naturally beautiful country you need to actually see it more frequently to raise your spirits.

On the same theme, I have a friend in her seventies who lives alone. Sometimes she awakes feeling rather lonely and less than happy. However, when she opens the curtains and reveals her wide, open garden, which catches the morning sunshine, she feels totally uplifted, simply thanks to nature doing what it does best.

Since we moved to our present home in 1972, I have occasionally discussed with Ruth what we really get from drawing back our curtains each morning and looking out over pretty gardens and leafy woodland. Now I realise that it is another contribution to our happy state of mind.

As an old friend of mine named Doug used to say with a glint in his ninety-two year old eye, 'Ain't nature wonderful.'

Above: Me with Jimmy Greaves; *Below:* Clive with Clive Allen

Above: Our garden in Kent; *Below:* Iguassu Falls in Brazil – Ain't nature wonderful

-20-

NOUGHT TO SIXTY IN NO TIME AT ALL

'And this our life, exempt from public haunt,
Finds tongues in trees, books in running brooks,
Sermons in stones, and good in everything.
I would not change it.'
(As You Like It by William Shakespeare, 1600)

Sixty years old is just the start, not the finishing line.

I decided to retire on my sixtieth birthday in March 2007. It was very easy and I miss nothing about my work or the people, who were mostly consultants and contractors. I regularly see one good friend Ian and his wife Sarah, who live in Kent, as well as Michael and Julie in the north-east. Even my finances worked out okay, what with a lump sum and pension. My accountant son sent me a really useful spreadsheet, in which I entered my income and expenditure projected until my ninetieth birthday. We will dip into savings each year, but not change our lifestyle one little bit and that makes me feel very content and secure.

In order to celebrate my birthday and retirement, we had an away weekend, relaxing with the family, if you call four grandchildren relaxing, especially when there is a swimming pool. One of the highlights was Ruth handing me a scrapbook, which she had crafted surreptitiously with entries from many members of my family, my good friends, work colleagues, school and university pals and, not least, our neighbours. She had previously made one of these for her brother's seventieth birthday and she realised how much I had admired it. Dave had managed to reach the end of his before bursting into tears, but I got very emotional and cried nearly all the way through mine. Luckily only Ruth was in the room when she handed it over. I shared it soon after with the family and subsequently sent my thanks to every contributor. People said some really sweet things which I will treasure, especially from my close family. I was kind of hoping they loved me and they said they did, so I will quote instead my pal from university days, Pete. He wrote that he considers me to be his 'first and best true (male) friend'. He generously claims that I influenced him in all sorts of ways, from my methodical approach to my pragmatism and my loyalty. He says I changed his life. Well, with his intelligence, honesty and ability to change, he made a big impact on me too!

As I mentioned in an earlier chapter, I retaliated eighteen months later by creating a scrapbook of Ruth's life to present at her special sixtieth birthday weekend with the family in September 2008. It took me eight months of secrecy and hiding my work-in-progress to complete the job, but I am very pleased with it. I tried to use as many craft techniques as Ruth had employed in my book and surprised everyone, not just Ruth, with the final product. It is not easy to put one over on somebody as sharp and clever as my wife! Once again there were super messages of love and admiration, with more than one expressing the fact that if they were to appear on 'Who Wants to be a Millionaire?' then Ruth would be their 'phone a friend'!

Pete said of us, 'They each seem to have provided a rock of stability and affection from which the other can face the world and its many trials with confidence'. Wow.

Friends approaching retirement have asked me how I tackled it and why I am so happy. Well, I made a list of all the things I wanted to do, prioritised them and simply got on with it. It was a mixture of household jobs, visiting my family and indulging in hobbies. I had put up a shed or 'Craft Barn' for Ruth's hobby of making things, at which she is brilliant, but I also fancied a large shed for myself. This made a total of four such buildings in the garden. A man cannot have too many sheds. Anyway, I slaved to clear a corner of the garden, levelled it nice and flat, then took possession of my enormous 'Sports Pavilion'. It contains a full size table-tennis table, a pool table and dart board. It is also a shrine to Tottenham Hotspur Football Club, containing all my memorabilia. I had removed these items from the house when I redecorated every room, which was another job I had on the list.

I will always keep up my exercise by running long distances, strolling around nature reserves and labouring in the garden. I am not paranoid about health issues, but for many years it has been natural for us to have at least five portions of fruit and vegetables a day, as well as oily fish two or three times a week. End of lecture, dear grandchildren.

I am also very happy to drive our lovely grandchildren around, as required, and do decorating or gardening for the family. However, I have recently added another activity, helping senior citizens! In July 2007 I went on a country walk with some old pals and one of them, Graham, who was almost eighty years old, asked whether I could give him a hand in his garden now and then. As far as I am concerned, chaps like him helped make Britain great and I am still helping him and his charming wife Margaret. However, at a garden party, Ruth and I met another very nice lady named Jean, got chatting and discovered that she also knew Graham. Serendipity again. I explained that I was helping him occasionally and she twisted my arm to give her a hand too. I am a bit of a soft touch, but I liked her positive outlook. Her late husband had owned a manufacturing firm employing a number of local people, so she deserved some support. I make sure that she and her property are looked after, as she and her husband had also been part of the backbone of our great country. Neither of these couples had been blessed with children and they need assistance from someone that they can trust. We should look after our older friends and neighbours. You can learn a great deal from them too. I know I have.

We also find it fun, as well as important, to maintain regular contact with our brothers and sisters, which we are achieving comfortably. Ruth's brother Dave sailed through a quadruple heart bypass and is as active as ever. When we visit him and Jean in Staffordshire, we are usually fortunate to see their children Mark and Nina too. It is also a pleasure to say that my dear sisters Colleen and Marilyn are very positive and find plenty to laugh about. My brother Gordon is not in the best of health, so has to take some care, but has a sweet and caring wife Carina, four great kids named Lloyd, Joe, Kelly and Debbie plus a growing collection of grandchildren, so I am very pleased for him.

One thing that I have done all my life, but have not mentioned yet is to smile. Experts say that simply by smiling you will feel happier, so think happy thoughts and try it. How you think affects how you feel, how you behave and how you appear to others, so let us try to pick out the positives in life and smile.

So, what is my legacy? What did I receive? How did I build on it? What will I pass on?

My parents gave me much love, good advice, the work ethic and their precious time.

Together with some massive help from Ruth, advice from friends and ideas that I have picked up along the way, I have tried to add a culture of helping others.

As well as enjoying travelling throughout Great Britain and around the world, I just adore my house and garden. It is safe, comfortable and my favourite place on the planet.

We built for our children a safe environment where they could express themselves, try new things and be happy. Education is vital and I am proud of what Clive and Kate have achieved. I am equally determined to do everything I can to support the education and happiness of my four delightful young grandchildren. If I live and breathe, I will do the same for their children too. Beyond that, it is fingers crossed that I can help my great-great grandchildren.

Legacies, like dynasties, have to carry on as naturally and effortlessly as possible. On his wedding day, my godson Paul asked me for the traditional godfatherly advice. It caught me by surprise. My answer may sound corny at first, but it was to 'simply love her'.

My happiness is the mutual love of my wife, helping my family, learning something every day, being organised, enjoying this beautiful world and writing this book.

So, here I am, proud, pleased and content with a legacy of love.

As happy as Larry.

Larry Brooks was born into a family of four children, renting the upstairs of a terraced house in Muswell Hill, north London. Despite very humble beginnings, he received excellent parental advice and a good education, which saw him build a career first in Information Technology, then the personal development of people.

Happily married to his childhood sweetheart Ruth for over forty years, they have two wonderful children and four delightful grandchildren.

Larry's many hobbies include natural history, running marathons and studying his ancestry. He is the 25 x great grandson of William the Conqueror and therefore a distant cousin of the Queen. He retired in 2007, is very busy and very happy. He would like everyone to find as much happiness as possible.

He is pictured in their favourite café in Folkestone with his mum, aged 90.

Lightning Source UK Ltd.
Milton Keynes UK
30 April 2010

153566UK00002B/46/P

9 781449 091149